The Complete Guide to
Climbing
(By Bike)
in Colorado

A guide to cycling climbing and the most difficult hill climbs in Colorado

John Summerson

Extreme Press
405 Kettle Court
Winston-Salem, NC 27104
336 659-7600
Extreme.press@yahoo.com

First Edition, May 2011

All photos by the author unless otherwise noted

Library of Congress Catalog Card Number: 2010939475

ISBN 13: 978-0-9792571-3-1

"The best climbers do not suffer less; they just suffer faster"

Chris Boardman

Front cover - The north side of Loveland Pass

Back cover - The top of East Portal; inset - Rist Canyon

Table of Contents

Northeast

Southeast

West

Preface

Colorado is certainly composed of varied terrain as it holds 10 national parks and monuments, 13 national forests and grasslands and 42 state parks which provide abundant opportunities for outdoor enthusiasts. But the first thing that comes to mind when one thinks of the Centennial State is mountains. Among the longest, highest and most beautiful in the World, the Rockies create many physical challenges. The other key element present within the state are its cyclists which may be the most avid and skilled group in the country. This combination produces a cycling atmosphere perhaps unlike anywhere else in the United States.

Having collected climb data from all over the United States while preparing the book 'The Complete Guide to Climbing By Bike' and with interest in climbing growing, I realized that many worthwhile hills were being left out of the nationwide guide simply because they were not among the very most difficult. This was particularly evident in Colorado which contains a large number of challenging, high altitude ascents.

While no one knows the local climbs better than those that live nearby, I think this database is comprehensive but likely not complete. At the least climbing data is now available in one place for those seeking this information. Today I still get a sense of satisfaction from finding another challenging hill to climb so please send any other Colorado climbs worthy of mention to the author for future editions.

Introduction

Road bike cycling is one of the most popular sports in the world and the biggest challenge within the sport, and its most intriguing aspect, is hill climbing. Major professional cycling tours such as the Tour de France are usually won and lost in the mountains. But why climb the hill? Climbing is also the most difficult part of cycling, requiring great energy and effort and on tough hills or going all out, producing pain. Why, then, do cyclists routinely engage in a painful activity that can result, as they themselves describe, in great suffering for the sole purpose of reaching the top?

In the case of professional riders it could be argued that they are paid to do it. For others answers may include losing weight, improving one's racing ability or fitness level, or getting back to where you started. But I think the real answer is because it's there. This simple phrase sums up the main reason people undertake physical challenges. Be it mountain climbing, distance running or peak-bagging by bike, the main reason cyclists will tolerate the pain is for the physical and mental challenge itself. Hills are there to be beaten.

For years, major cycling events such as the Tour de France have evoked the image of the lone rider struggling up sheer alpine pitches, straining their physical limits. Cycling greats such as Eddy Merckx, Bernard Hinault and Lance Armstrong, while very complete all-around riders, became legends in the sport in large part from their climbing exploits. The mountains add an almost mythic quality to races as the riders are seen overcoming obstacles that extend beyond the actual asphalt, rock and dirt upon which they climb. Even average cyclists feel the allure of attempting difficult climbs and achieve tremendous satisfaction from a successful summit. It sounds pretty simple. Find a mountain with a paved road to the top and then pedal up it. However, hill climbing is not easy, as certain climbs involve ascents of thousands of vertical feet. Elite riders can race to the top but success for most involves just getting there.

As Colorado has many challenging hills to conquer, this book is meant to be a resource for road bike hill climbing and to describe the most difficult paved climbs in the state. Other ascents are included for reasons such as a steep grade or some other unique aspects.

The beginning of the climb to Mount Evans

Climbing

No one may know when the first significant hill was climbed on a bicycle but the first documentation of major ascents occurred in stage races which originated in Europe, the oldest being the Tour de France. It is interesting to note that the first two Tours (first held in 1903) did not include any mountain passes. Bikes were heavy, single speed (and brake) behemoths while many roads were unpaved. Some felt that the riders of the day could not complete big climbs and that adding them to the race route would ruin the Tour.

It was not until 1905 that significant climbs were added, the very first being the Ballon d'Alsace in the Vosges Mountains. In 1910 the first major, high altitude passes were added (four major climbs in the Pyrenees Mountains including the now famous Tourmalet) which resulted in a great deal of criticism directed at race organizers that the routes were too difficult. As is often the case human potential was underestimated as many riders of that era conquered the climbs in dramatic fashion. In contrast, 1910 was also the year that the broom wagon was introduced to sweep riders up who could not finish the stage.

In 1911 the first major climb in the Alps was added (Col de Galibier) with spectacular results. Instead of being a detriment, the uphill duels captured the public imagination and added to the popularity of the event. The race route every year thereafter has contained many significant climbs. Other major tours that followed also began to include hills along their routes. In 1933 the Tour de France and the Giro d'Italia (Italy's national tour) began recognizing the best climbers in the field (Spain's Vicente Trueba was the first winner in the Tour along with Alfredo Binda in the Giro). Most major stage races now recognize this accomplishment as the cyclists earn points based upon their climb finish and its difficulty. The cyclist with the most points is awarded the Polka Dot Jersey as the winner of the king of the mountains competition.

The performances of great early climbers such as Alfredo Binda, Fausto Coppi and Charley Gaul continued to increase the popularity of the major tours. These events made climbs such as the Tourmalet and L'Alpe d'Huez in France and Stelvio in Italy as well known to cycling fans as the Daytona Speedway or Yankee Stadium are to U.S. racing and baseball fans respectively. The mountains allowed bike races to become truly great as the event rose beyond the personal concerns of the cyclists to reflect life as a whole.

Today hill climbing is more popular than ever and within multi-stage races those with hilltop finishes are usually the most anticipated and best attended stages of the race. Racing fans know that hills offer the best opportunity to view the drama within the peloton as it struggles through the most difficult and important element in any race. Climbing adds the mythic quality of overcoming obstacles that is associated with the major cycling tours and which has produced many memorable moments. Ascending difficult hills is about struggle and perseverance and it is these aspects that have made conquering the mountains the heart and soul of cycling.

About This Guidebook

Road bike cycling and hill climbing in particular are enjoying a surge in popularity in the U.S., perhaps due to the success of the major road bike races and Lance Armstrong and/or the ongoing fitness/physical challenge craze in this country. In spite of growing popularity however, there is little published information on the location of area road bike hill climbs and very little accurate data on the length and elevation gain of these climbs. Many roads are hilly but that is not the intent of this guide. The location, description and profiling of major individual paved hills in Colorado is its aim. As such, I set out to publish a guide for those cyclists looking for this information and to collect data for climb comparison purposes. You will have some of these hills all to yourself at times as they are not well known.

In addition to listing the location of climbs I wanted to provide accurate data on their length, grade, elevation gain and other statistics. While there are various data available it is important when compiling data to reduce the variability of measurement that can occur from multiple sources and to apply consistent definitions to hill climbs. The listed statistics for climbs often vary as different people use different starting and ending points and less than accurate measurement procedures. At times climb gradients are reported inaccurately or overestimated such as when the maximum grade is sometimes considered the average grade. In addition, climbs are sometimes profiled by using mapping software to analyze roads that have been superimposed upon a topographic map. Roads are at times not accurately laid down within map contours which can result in less than accurate measurements. The measurements in this guide were all obtained directly on each climb and compiled by one source.

There are hundreds of climbs in and around the mountains of Colorado so obviously they all cannot be included in these pages. What this guidebook does include are the most difficult paved road bike climbs in the state (see appendices for rankings). Other climbs are described due to a steep grade, or other unique aspect such as outstanding scenery (along with significant climbing), cycling history or some combination of the above. Appendices in this guide rank climbs by overall difficulty, average grade, elevation gain and several other categories. The author has first hand knowledge of 99 out of the 101 (98%) described climbs in this guide. Those with estimated statistics are noted. It is a difficult task to attempt to record and document all of the significant climbs in Colorado so if noteworthy ascents were left out please send the appropriate information to the author.

While some of the ascents in this guide are for the serious road cyclist only, there are many moderate climbs for the rider looking to improve their climbing skills and/or fitness level. Be sure to know your fitness and ability level before you tackle the longer and/or more difficult hills in this book. Start with the shorter, less steep climbs and progress from there. As all are located in the mountains, the scenery along the way is usually spectacular and will help ease the pain of a tough ascent.

Near the top of Rist Canyon near Fort Collins

The west side of Independence Pass

Defining A Hill Climb

Along with the location and statistics of Colorado climbs, this guide will attempt to standardize the definition of a hill climb. That is, what constitutes a climb, what are the starting and ending points and, if multiple approaches, the shortest route to the top. The start and finish of most climbs are generally easy to define as they have definite beginnings and endings. Others are a bit vague, particularly along shallow-grade stretches of road. The starting point of these types of climbs is considered to be the transition from flat to a definite climb or a significant change in elevation for very gently climbing stretches of roads. A good example of the latter is the north side of Red Mountain Pass along Route 550 (one of the most spectacular climbs in the U.S.). Route 550 actually begins to climb many miles to the north of its listed start in Ouray, CO. However, the grade is so slight that the author believes this should not be considered a hill climb. Once in Ouray it is quite clear where the true hill begins as there is a significant change in grade right in the middle of town.

Another topic worthy of discussion regarding climb definitions is a clarification of their ending points. Most climbs have an easy-to-define end such as Mount Mitchell in North Carolina which dead-ends very close to the top of the mountain. However, some do not. For climbs that do not dead end, the top is considered when the road descends from that point (such as mountain passes), or if it reaches a significant flat without significant climbing beyond it. A good example of the latter is Sunshine Canyon near Boulder. At its listed top the road flattens out. Over the next few miles the road rolls up and down before peaking at an altitude that is slightly higher than the listed climb peak. However, the additional climbing is not constant and is over such shallow grade that the additional riding does not constitute climbing in the author's mind.

Another issue in defining climbs is how flat sections and/or descents along the route factor in. A climb can have small flats and/or infrequent small descents and still be considered a continuous ascent as long as the vast majority of the route is uphill (< 10% of the route is flats/ descents). Many major hill climbs have small descents along the way but these sections always lead to significant additional climbing. Some very good rides with serious elevation gain however contain multiple flats/descents and are not included. These would include Route 130 in South Carolina; a very entertaining ride that climbs a significant distance but that has too much of its route along flat and/or descending terrain.

Some climbs may have a single major flat/descent (no more than one mile in length) if there is extended, significant climbing both before and after the flat/descent. For example, Mount Mitchell in North Carolina has a single major descent along its route but because there is significant climbing both before and after the descent it is considered a single climb. If a climb has more than one major flat/descent along its route it is considered two separate climbs. For instance, Route 168 from Fresno toward Kaiser Pass in California has more than 8000 feet of elevation gain along its route but there are several major descents along the way so the route is actually several different climbs. Mount Hamilton near San Jose, California is another example; it contains three uphill sections between two fairly major descents and while the climbing sections are worthy in themselves, the route from bottom to top is not considered by most to be one hill climb.

Definitions of Terms

This guide will use several terms to describe each climb which are defined below:

Total elevation - This is the elevation gained in feet from the starting point to the top of the climb. If a climb has descents within it this additional climbing is not included in the total elevation gained. Elevations were measured using global positioning satellite (GPS) positions from which a very accurate elevation was then determined by plotting the fixed point using a topographic software program.

Length - This is the distance of the climb in miles. If you are retracing your route back to the starting point, in order to determine the total distance of the ride, simply double the climb's length. Climb lengths were measured by automobile odometer (at least two measures and averaged) and cycle computer.

Average Grade (maximum grade) - This is the average percent grade or steepness of the climb and is expressed as a percentage (8%). The grade assigned to each hill is the average grade over the entire climb. The higher the percent grade, the steeper the climb. Percent grade is determined by dividing the elevation gain by the length of the climb. The maximum grade is just that. The measured maximum gradient must extend all the way across the road (a very steep inside corner that could be bypassed for instance does not qualify) and be at least ten feet in length. Maximum gradient was measured by gradiometer. In the listed climb descriptions the distance and elevation

Colorado National Monument

Steep grade on Cottonwood Pass

data only reflect the contiguous portion of the road that is part of the climb. If the climb includes small flats or descents, they are included in the distance but do not contribute to the net elevation gain. Thus the average grade may not in some cases accurately represent the true nature of the climb. That is, there are usually sections on the climb that are steeper than the average grade along with sections that are less steep than the average grade.

Rating - There are several formulas available to rank climbs. All have shortcomings and have received criticism. In major races such as the Tour de France climbs are ranked using a numeric scale from 4 (easiest) to 1 with an extra classification describing the most difficult climbs as hors categoire or 'beyond category'. There are general guidelines for these categorizations that involve length and grade. However there are not precise definitions for each category and often the ratings are not applied consistently. In addition, climbs are often ranked according to their placement within a race stage meaning that a climb towards the end of a stage may be categorized as a 2 when the same climb may be a 3 (easier) if placed at the beginning of the stage. You may also have noticed that more recently certain climbs used in the Tour de France have been receiving a more difficult rating than for previous tours (call it hill inflation perhaps), regardless of their placement in a stage. The elevation reached within a climb is not taken into account in this and most other ratings systems as well. As increasing elevation has deleterious effects on physical performance, this factor should be taken into consideration. The point here is that a more accurate formula is needed and the one listed below is an attempt to more precisely quantify the difficulty of a climb and has taken into account the climb's elevation gain, average grade, altitude, surface and grade variability:

Average grade x total elevation gain x altitude adjustment (see altitude adjustment description) x grade variability (see grade variability adjustment description).

Altitude adjustment: Altitude research indicates that human performance shows a noticeable performance detriment beginning at approximately 2000 feet elevation of approximately 1% with subsequent performance deficits with increasing altitude and duration of activity. There are other elements that affect performance at altitude but vary by individual and at this point in time are very difficult if not impossible to quantify. The author acknowledges that the adjustment presented here is an estimation of the effects of altitude on performance.

Grade variability adjustment: If a climb has two or more segments where the grade of the segment exceeds the average climb grade by at least five percentage points the rating is adjusted by 0.025 (assumption that grade variability results in a slightly more difficult climb) for each of those sections. Very few climbs meet this criterion.

As you can see from the climb rankings there is very little difference in the numeric rating of many of the climbs. So little in fact that you will have a very difficult time discerning the differences while on the bike. All that having been said, there are too many variables involved to precisely rank a climb numerically and it is not the main intent of this guide to do so. While the author believes this rating system is an improvement over other models it is hoped that these ratings, while serving as a general guide to compare climbs, will also serve to spur debate and perhaps eventually a truly accurate rating system.

Directions - The starting point for almost all directions for climbs listed in this guidebook is the nearest town, some of which are very tiny places. A good road map will be helpful to locate and reach many of these locations. I would recommend the North American Road Atlas from AAA as it contains a town index for each state but any national/state highway road map will do.

Rules of the Road

- Wear a helmet.
- Follow the same driving rules as motorists and be sure to obey all traffic patterns and road signs.
- Wear bright colors so you are more visible to motorists.
- Ride single file on busy roads so that motorized vehicles can pass.
- Use hand signals to alert motorists to your next move.
- Ride with traffic and not against it.
- Make eye contact with drivers and assume they do not see you.
- Try to avoid riding in foggy, rainy or windy conditions.
- In summer ride early on high altitude ascents to avoid thunder storms and down slope winds during afternoons
- Be alert for sewer grates, manhole covers, cattle guards,

oily pavement, gravel, wet leaves and ice.

- Give parked cars a wide berth.
- Many of these listed climbs are fairly long rides so go prepared with an extra tube along with pump, tool kit, rain gear, food and plenty of fluids at all times.
- It is usually best to ride with a partner or partners.In case of emergency one rider can go for help if needed.

Pre-Ride Check

- Check the tires for proper inflation.
- Check the brakes for proper traction.
- Check all quick releases to make sure they are tight.
- Check the chain for tightness.
- Check all nuts and bolts.
- Spin your wheels through frame and brakes.
- Make sure you have all necessary gear for the particular climb/ride.
- Bring a positive attitude along whenever possible.

Improving Climbing Ability

For new cyclists, hill climbing is one of the most daunting aspects of riding. More experienced cyclists, however, enjoy climbing and regard tough hills as a challenge. It is a great feeling to make a solid climb and then enjoy the descent down the other side. The simplest way to improve your climbing technique and the best training for climbing is to climb; that is, to incorporate hills into your rides. However, don't start climbing big hills until you have built up an adequate cycling fitness base. Try to accumulate a significant amount of relatively flat riding first. At that point add shorter/moderate grade hills to your rides and work your way up to the longer and/or steeper climbs. Incorporating hills in your riding will not make them any shorter but eventually they will feel that way.

Cycling Techniques for Climbing

Improving your basic cycling techniques can also improve your climbing ability. It is important to maintain a smooth, steady rhythm as you pedal up the hill. Unless very short in length, start a climb with as slow a pace as possible. This will allow you to develop a rhythm which not only includes the pedaling cadence but breathing as well. Breathe slowly and deeply as this will help establish a smooth pedaling cadence. Obviously in your pedal stroke it is much easier to apply force to the pedals when your foot is on the down stroke. However, this results in uneven power output contributing to slight accelerations and decelerations of the bike which becomes exaggerated when climbing. To remedy this try to lift your knee and

Exposure high on Mount Evans

Riders descend Lookout Mountain near Golden

drag your foot backwards across the bottom of the pedal stroke, pulling upwards slightly on the upstroke and pulling the pedal forward across the top of its rotation.

There are several other factors to consider when climbing. First, make sure you have the right gears. At least a 39-tooth small chain ring in front and a 25-tooth rear gear (a 27 or 28 is even better if you will be riding consistently on steep hills). Upon encountering a hill, do not shift too soon as this can result in a momentum loss from a high RPM spinning effect. Conversely, you must not end up in a gear that is too large which tends to tire the rider out. The proper climbing cadence varies among individuals. The idea with gearing is to maintain a cadence that is comfortable, shifting as you tire and the RPM's start to drop. Basically, if the gradient varies on the climb adjust your gearing so that your cadence and level of effort are maximized.

Another factor is whether to sit or stand during the ascent. Seated is more energy efficient but a standing position can produce much more power. A simple rule to start with is that if the hill is long, climb in the saddle, and if short or while attacking, stand. Reality dictates that on most challenging hills you will do both. For most of the climb you will find it is more efficient to sit in the saddle. Put your hands on the top of the brake hoods or handlebars and keep them relaxed. Try to change their positioning periodically. The upper body should not be crunched forward too far and the shoulders should be open. This will allow for easier breathing as the climb continues. Relax your upper body as well, as this will decrease oxygen demands. Your weight should be over the cranks to maximize power during the pedal stroke. Try not to bounce on the pedals as you shift from side to side. Developing a rhythm that combines pedaling and breathing will make a big difference in your climbing efficiency. At times you will need to stand such as on very steep sections or when sprinting past a fellow rider. Just before you stand, shift to a higher gear as you can generate more power in this position (shift back when you sit down again). As you come off of the saddle continue with an even pedal stroke and push your hands forward. Come out of the saddle on the down stroke to minimize loss of momentum.

Specific Training for Hill Climbing

While the physiology of human performance training is much more understood today than in the past, training is still as much art as science. That is, there is more than one way to improve performance. However, perhaps the more important considerations are time and commitment. Time to train is obviously limited for most. With that in mind it is paramount that this limited time is put to good use. Intensity is the key with adequate rest for recovery. Particularly with hill climbing which involves very intense bursts of effort, adequate recovery is essential to avoid overtraining and burnout. In addition, train consistently for best results. Develop specific climbing goals and a plan to reach those goals. Listen to your body and back off if needed. Commit to climbing success and it will likely follow.

Good climbers have certain attributes that contribute to their success. All have an endurance base and have developed solid power to weight ratios which gives the ability to generate greater amounts of force with each pedal stroke. They also have high anaerobic endurance which results in greater levels of lactic acid tolerance. Training to improve climbing ability should focus on these physiologic aspects.

Build a Base

As previously mentioned make sure you have a solid cycling base before adding significant climbing to your riding and attempting the interval routines described later in this section. You should complete many miles of distance riding on mostly flat terrain to build your endurance base before moving on to more specialized routines that target climbing ability. The amount of time needed will vary by individual, ranging from several months to several years of regular road cycling depending on age, health and fitness level. After a period of mainly flat riding, add moderate hills to your regular endurance rides. As you progress, add longer and steeper hills.

Power to Weight Ratio

Climbing ability has a strong correlation with power to weight ratio; in fact it is perhaps the most accurate predictor of climbing success. As you may have noticed, the climbing specialists on the pro tour are almost all very lean (the late Marco Pantani comes to mind). Thus, climbing can be improved by increasing power, losing body weight or, for the greatest results, a combination of the two. Even a relatively small weight loss (3-5 lbs) can produce significant improvement. Much information is available regarding losing weight so this guide will not attempt to add to that body of knowledge. Just keep in mind that weight loss can lead to reductions in power

Difficult East Portal near Montrose

The start of steep Magnolia Road

output (to maintain power lose as much fat and as little muscle as possible). Increasing cycling power will be touched upon in the following sections and comes about through specific training.

Regarding the advantages of lower weight, do not forget your bike. As long as component stiffness is not compromised (stiffer rims and frames flex less during use and thus take less energy to push up hills) reducing your machine's weight will improve its ability to climb as well. Rotating weight is the real key so you will see the biggest gains from reductions in this area. Use the lightest rims, pedals and shoes you can afford. Tires with smoother and thinner treads and stronger sidewalls will also help.

Improving Lactate Threshold

Lactate threshold is the point at which lactic acid begins to accumulate above moderate levels, resulting in fatigue in the affected muscles. This quickly results in the inability to continue to perform at this level of work. Most riders know the heavy legged feeling after a hard bout of work when you must slow down in order to keep going. The goal of training is to raise the point at which lactic acid accumulates enough to affect performance. All things being equal, the higher your lactate threshold, the faster the pace you can hold on climbs. While lactate threshold can be measured directly it correlates well with heart rate and is normally between 75-90% of maximum heart rate. The goal of climbing-specific training should be to increase that percentage towards the top of the range. A simple way to estimate your lactate threshold is to perform two bouts of work. When rested and motivated and after a good warm-up, perform a twenty minute time trial at

maximum effort and record your average heart rate. Repeat this test under similar conditions. The average heart rate for both efforts is a close approximation of your heart rate at your lactate threshold. Providing you have a sufficient aerobic endurance base (see 'Build a Base' above) lactate threshold training should improve your climbing ability. This is very demanding training however and will require proper recovery between bouts so don't forget to include easy days on the bike when needed.

Interval Routines

A very effective way to increase your power and to raise your lactate threshold in order to improve climbing ability is through the use of intervals. Intervals are relatively short bursts of more intense effort followed by a recovery period. Several of the below routines should be interspersed (start at the top of the below list and progress down) within your regular riding training (1-3 times per week) depending upon the season. Use them more frequently for pre-season training; tapering off before races. Add/delete routines as needed. Recovery between intervals should be easy, high cadence spinning on mostly level ground.

Big gear climbs - On various hill grades shift up one cog from normal (harder gear) for 1-2 minutes. Keep cadence at least 50 RPM and stay seated.

Cruise intervals - 3 to 5 intervals for 6-12 minutes each on a moderate grade (3-5%) at or just below your lactate threshold. Recover for 2-4 minutes. Gradually add minutes to each interval.

Anaerobic endurance intervals - 3-5 intervals for 2-4 minutes each on a 6-8% grade, gradually building the intensity, with cadence of at least 60 RPM. Intensity should be above your lactate threshold for the second half of the interval. Recovery should be double the interval length.

Extended Climbing at Lactate Threshold - On a steady and moderate grade, climb for 15-30 minutes at or just slightly above your lactate threshold. Gradually add minutes up to 30 (or the longest hill you may need to climb).

Sit/Stand intervals - On a moderate hill and at a comfortable cadence, alternate seated and standing climbing of equal intervals. After thirty seconds in the saddle, stand on the pedals for 30 seconds. After another minute of climbing in the saddle, stand for one minute, etc. Gradually build the intervals up to 4-5 minutes each.

Hill Sprints - Perform 5-10 sprints for 10-15 seconds at maximum effort. Gradually move from moderate to steeper hills. Recover for five minutes between each sprint.

Hill Jumps - While climbing a moderate hill do 4-5 sets of 3-5 jumps for ten crank turns (both feet) at max effort. Recover for one minute between each jump and five minutes between sets.

Advanced Hill Jumps - On a moderate grade perform 3-5 two minute sets, attacking every thirty seconds for ten pedal strokes. Stand for the attacks which should be at maximum effort; stay seated otherwise. Recover for five minutes between sets.

Weight Training

One factor linked to climbing success is leg strength. Particularly if you cannot put in year round riding on hills, weight training sessions should be added to your weekly routine. Ideally hit the weight room 2-3 times per week in the off season and once per week in season, tapering off before races or big rides. Increasing upper body strength has the potential to reduce upper body fatigue and increasing lower body strength will give you the ability to push a bigger gear over the same hill. The below exercises will give you the most benefit for your time spent in the gym. Do not include both squats and leg presses unless leg strength is a very weak area. Masters riders or those with lower back issues should not include squats in their routine and should perform the leg press instead.

Squat - 2-3 sets of 8-12 repetitions

Leg press - 2-3 sets of 8-12 repetitions

Calf raise - 2-3 sets of 8-12 repetitions

Step-ups - 2-3 sets of 8-12 repetitions

Bench press - 2-3 sets of 8-12 repetitions

Lat pulldown - 2-3 sets of 8-12 repetitions

Push-ups - 2-3 sets of 25 repetitions

Sit-ups (crunches) - 2-3 sets of 25 repetitions

Back extensions - 2-3 sets of 25 repetitions

Descending

Descending ability, like any other skill, is best obtained and improved with practice. The more time you can spend on descending, the more confidence and speed you will be able to develop. The most important aspect of descending is relaxation. Anxiety can narrow your concentration and you may end up missing a dangerous aspect of the road ahead. Speed is obviously important but pushing your speed to the point of fear will not help your descending skills. Work on relaxation and speed will follow. Keep a slight bend in the arms and slide back in the saddle, keeping your hands on the drops of your bars. One important riding habit to develop is to look far enough in front of you to match the pace at which you are descending. During a faster descent you need to watch the road much further in front of the bike. Set up well in advance of a curve and do whatever braking needs to done before entering the turn. If you are riding in a group, spread out. This will allow each rider to take their preferred line through the corners; critical in that you may not have time to adjust once you commit. It also allows a greater margin if a rider needs to brake. For long descents you should use both brakes equally. Once in a turn any traction used for braking significantly reduces the traction available for cornering.

In wet conditions the distance required to stop is extended. Lightly apply the brakes periodically on a wet descent to remove excess water from the rims. Compete only against yourself on a fast descent and exercise caution on unfamiliar roads by always being prepared for road debris or traffic around every blind corner. In many cases descents are followed by another climb; if so, try to spin the pedals as you approach the bottom so

The west side of Rist Canyon

Views from Flagstaff Mountain near Boulder

that you will be warmed up for the next section of riding. Take it easy, relax, concentrate on the road, and most importantly, practice descending, and you will find your skills improving.

Mental Training

As professional cyclist Chris Boardman once said "The best climbers do not suffer less, they just suffer faster". Climbing is painful, suffering the name of the game. That said there may also be some less conventional ways to improve your climbing ability. Developing mental focus to enable one to block out distractions, including physical discomfort, is another attribute of good climbers and should be included in your training regimen. All negative thoughts must go during workouts or races. The minute you think you cannot make a climb is when you may get dropped. Many riders are dropped on climbs before they reach their physical breaking point simply because of negative thoughts.

Begin working on mental focus by clearing your mind entirely. This can be a difficult skill to master but can be developed in stretches during long rides. Be patient as it sometimes takes time to see progress. Once this skill is developed begin to think of a single thought or image. Try to keep this single thought or image in your mind for extended periods. Once you have developed this ability you will find it much easier to concentrate over a climb. Work on visualizing images of light or soaring objects as you work your way up the hill. These images can lower the perception of effort. Even if climbing times are similar the effect should be one of additional energy for the remainder of the race or ride. Remember, everyone suffers on a tough climb. Climbing can be as much a mental as physical challenge, so try not to let a lack of self-confidence affect your performance. Developing ways to deal mentally with the physical aspects of getting over tough hills should produce better results on the road.

Climbing Tactics

There are some specific strategies regarding climbing that can have dramatic results when it comes to better race finishes. First of all, as with the overall route, it pays to be very familiar with the climbs along the way, so scout major hills if at all possible, noting the position of flat or very steep sections, particularly those that are stage/race finishes. When many inexperienced riders come to a hill they simply go all out and feel tremendous pressure to reach the top. Unless it is the last climb of the day doing so results in spending enormous amounts of energy that could be saved for the finish. Until you are a great climber you should maintain your own pace. Trying to stay with the top climbers is not good strategy. Instead try to find the exact personal pace that will help you cut your losses. Never ride faster than you know you can go. If needed, as you get comfortable with the climb, see if you can pick up the pace over the last half so that by the top you can catch the original group with which you started. You may be surprised by how many riders you pass along the way. Ideally try to time the effort so that you catch the pack at the summit. Unless you are the first over the top, be careful not to slow down near summits that are not race finishes. As the leaders begin to accelerate on the descent each rider has to push harder over the top in order to hold the wheel in front of him. Shift into a bigger gear as you approach the summit and accelerate over the top. You can recover on the descent from the extra effort involved.

Riders who are good sprinters often come to a hill in or near the lead and then drift to the back of the pack during the climb. On the descent and any following flats they can often catch the lead group before the next climb. By doing this several times early in a ride/race you can save a lot of energy for the finish while also developing the confidence of knowing that you do not have to crest climbs near the front to be successful. If the climb is the last of the day, obviously your tactics will need to change. You may need to make an all out effort to catch the lead group such as when the finish is very close or if being with the group will save a lot of energy (long, flat section just ahead). As you gain experience and become more aware of group dynamics you will start to make better decisions earlier in a climb and save energy as well.

Once you become a good climber, attack on the hills. Use your strength to put time on your competitors as you may need it over the remainder of the race/ride. An early attack can keep pressure on those who may be stronger in other areas. Riders that push too hard trying to keep up with you on a hill early in the race may find themselves struggling on the last climb of the day. Steeper sections are often a good place to launch an attack as you can more quickly open a gap before other riders react. However, attacking early on a hilly stage is a risky decision as you will either ride to victory or go down in flames if the peloton swallows you up before the finish. Depending on the result your decision will be portrayed as courageous or foolish bravado so if you go make sure you are committed to the move. Many a cyclist has made

The north side of Loveland Pass

Double digit grade near Fort Collins

a name for themselves breaking away on a monster climb and staying away so don't let a prior failed attempt keep you from trying again.

If the race finish is the hill crest obviously it is best to be out in front by a comfortable margin and cruise to victory up the final climb. However, until you are a super climber that situation may rarely present itself. Unless it is a very long climb get into the lead group as soon as possible. Once there, knowing when to attack is a crucial skill to master. Much of your decision will be based on how you are feeling that day and on race conditions and will become clearer with additional climbing/racing experience. The other contending riders may also come into play. If there is a sprinter in the lead group you may want to go early and take his legs out from under him. If so, take a measured approach. Launch an attack but not an all out effort. Even though part of the group may stay with you, the effort should drop a few riders. If you are feeling good continue the attack. If you are able to continue at a relatively high cadence you should drop all but the strongest climbers. Unless you have ridden all riders off of your wheel it will come down to your placement in the group and timing as the finish line draws near. The first thing you must do is know where the finish line is. If you scouted the hill even if the last section is twisty with obscured views you should have an advantage. Once you have a good idea of how far away the line is, positioning will be key. Draft off other riders as much as possible as you approach the summit. When the finish is in sight try to be the second or third wheel before the final sprint begins. Realize this is easier said than done and knowing how to position within the group will again come from experience. The time to start your finishing sprint will depend upon your sprinting ability. The greater your sprinting skills, the earlier you can launch your assault. Always be alert for the rider in front of you moving first. Come out of the saddle on the down stroke as you make your move. Once you pull away try to stay directly in front of the rest of the pack so they will have to move around you to pass. Don't look back as you power toward the line. All of these actions should be thought out well before the actual finishing stretch. Many of these tactical maneuvers come with experience so train with experienced riders to see how they approach climbs, or shadow a particular rider, noting how they adjust to different situations on the hill.

Summary

To get the most out of the time on your bike and to avoid overtraining refer to the below summary:

- Build a strong aerobic base before adding a lot of climbing mileage to your training rides
- Add climbing to your regular training rides
- Utilize interval training to improve climbing ability
- Build up the intensity of your training slowly
- Train consistently for best results
- Eat a balanced diet
- Try to get a minimum of eight hours sleep every night
- Set short, medium and long-term goals
- Use a training diary and review when needed
- Know yourself and adjust your workouts accordingly

- Don't forget to include easy days on the bike if you are including extensive climbing routines in your training
- Use mental techniques to develop positive thoughts during climbing
- Practice descending skills to round out your mountain training
- Don't forget the tactical side of climbing

The top of Bonham Reservoir

Memorable Climbing Performances

There have been many amazing climbing performances over the years, the most publicized having taken place in Europe. These performances are too numerous to list here and are well documented in other places. From the dominating mountain stage wins of Alfredo Binda, Gino Bartali, Fausto Coppi and Charly Gaul in the early European tours to the death of Tim Simpson on Mount Venous and other more contemporary battles among the legends of the sport including Eddy Merckx, Bernard Hinault, Greg Lemond, Marco Pantani and Lance Armstrong, there are many stories to tell. Exclusively American climbing exploits have a fairly short, but accomplished history, mainly contained within the last thirty years or so. The stories presented here have an American theme (either by rider or location) and while some are well known many may be unknown to all but the most die-hard cycling fan.

There are so many tales to tell that all cannot be expanded upon, including some of the early Red Zinger/ Coors Classic stage race battles in the Rockies, European race exploits such as Greg Lemond's wins in the 1980 Circuit de la Sarthe and 1983 World Championship, Alexi Grewal's mountain stage win in the 1984 Tour de l'Avenir, the 1986 and 1987 Tour of Switzerland wins over difficult terrain by Andy Hampsten, and the Blue Ridge and Appalachian Mountain performances in the now defunct Tour du Pont. Others worthy of mention but not included in these pages are the victories by Moninger,

Vaughters and Wherry in the now defunct Red Zinger/ Saturn Classic, one of the most difficult one day races in the world (held in Colorado from 2000-2002), Lance Armstrong's uphill time trial win to capture the 2001 Tour of Switzerland, his queen (most difficult) stage win in the 2001 Tour de France that gave him the overall race lead or the two mountain stage victories that contributed mightily to his 2002 TdF win. In addition, the exploits of climbers in the recently inaugurated Everest Challenge, a two day stage race in California that has the greatest elevation to mileage ratio for any U.S. race, are not touched upon as well as many others due to lack of space or detailed information. Listed chronologically, those listed here are performances that are among the most significant in American cycling climbing history.

Top of the World

Mount Evans in Colorado is one of the most difficult hill climbs in the world. With a beginning elevation well above 7000 feet, the paved road on its slopes reaches heights greater than any outside of the Himalayas or Andes Mountains. It is also home to the oldest climbing race in the U.S., first held in 1962. Winning this very difficult race, with its unparalleled altitude attained, is a testament to climbing ability. The winner list is one of great American climbers and includes Alexi Grewal, Ned Overend, Jonathan Vaughters, and Tom Danielson. One win in this prestigious event would be a worthy achievement for any top level rider. Multiple wins signify a truly great climber. Winning the overall title each time it was held from 1975-1980, American Bob Cook also set the course

The east side of Route 96

Descending in the Rockies

record four times in that span. Tragically, Bob Cook passed away in 1981 at the age of twenty-three. The race is now named in memorial for the first five time winner of the event who many consider perhaps the best American climber of any era. Mike Engleman also won the race five times in a row from 1991 to 1995, an equally incredible feat. Scott Moninger has won this race an amazing six times which is quite an achievement. Winning this difficult race multiple times deserves to be considered among the most impressive of climbing feats.

Rocky Mountain High

The Coors Classic (formerly the Red Zinger Classic) was America's first top level stage race and one of the most influential cycling events on this continent. Attracting the world's best riders, it allowed many Americans to see top flight competitive cycling for the first time. Held mainly in Colorado, it always contained many hill climbs within a high altitude environment. In the 1981 version the top team entered was from the Soviet Union. Even though they were technically an amateur team (members did not receive any prize money but were fully supported by the Soviet government and thus could train full time) they were as good as the best professional teams of that era. This was evident in the precise teamwork of its cyclists. Once the Soviet train got moving and was working at its peak it was riding everyone off of its wheels. However, there was one exception. A young man from Nevada who was just starting to make waves in the cycling world was also entered in the Coors Classic that year. Having won several prestigious American titles, he was able to stay with the Soviets, and any other riders for that matter, through the difficult terrain. Greg Lemond, despite having a weak team, stayed with the mighty Soviets throughout the high altitude rides and climbs of the Rockies, pulling ahead at the end of several stages to win. Essentially winning the race single handedly, his impressive mountain performance was a prelude to major tour victories on cycling's most hallowed grounds.

The Future

The Tour de l'Avenir (Tour of the Future) held in France each year is a 10-day stage race sponsored by the Tour de France for top amateurs and young professional riders. It is also similar to the TdF in that it contains plenty of climbing and top flight competition. In 1982 the field was one of the strongest ever including the best national teams in the world along with some of the top up and coming European pros. In addition, a team from Columbia was entered that contained some of the best climbers on the planet. The team from East Germany dominated the early, flat stages but things began to change in Stage 4. This stage was a short mountain time trial and it was here that that the future arrived as American Greg Lemond rode to victory, picking up eighteen seconds on the second place rider. The next day's stage was a brutal one including climb after climb along the route and ending with a hilltop finish. The Columbian team attacked early and often but Lemond followed each one. Toward the end of the stage he opened up a gear that would later be seen winning the Tour de France as he pulled away from everyone and crushed the stage, winning by over five minutes. Greg Lemond ended up winning the Tour de l'Avenir by more than ten minutes, becoming the first and only American ever to do so and building on a record that would become one of the best in the history of the sport.

The Women's Movement

In 1984 the Tour de France held the first Tour for women. Because of the Olympics being held in Los Angeles later that summer the U.S. did not send an official team (and its best riders) to the event. Instead a bicycle club from New Jersey sent a small group to represent the country. Without a coach or national uniforms (they also rode on borrowed bikes) the group headed to France not without a bit of trepidation. Once the race began over mostly flat stages, the Tour was dominated by a strong Dutch team. The last rider picked for the American effort, Marianne Martin, used these early stages to ride herself into top shape. By the time Stage 14 rolled around Martin was ready to make her move. The stage was a difficult one, essentially one long hill and ending at the top of a ski resort. Martin pulled away right from the start and went on to win the stage by almost four minutes, an amazing margin of victory considering the stage was only twenty miles long. Picking up the yellow jersey as race leader as well at the end of that day, she held on all the way to Paris to become the first winner of the Tour de France Feminin.

Steep going ahead

Desolate terrain above 12,000 feet

Conquering the Colombian Heights

Despite its endemic poverty and violence, the country of Colombia, with its towering mountains, has somehow managed to produce a storied cycling history. With some of the toughest riding conditions in the world it is a very inhospitable place for foreign riders; rebuffing even the great Fausto Coppi late in his career. Full of very high elevation passes as well as many of the best climbers in the world (in fact, Colombian Luis Herrera is the only rider to win the King of the Mountains title outright in all three major tours), Colombia held the annual Caracol de la Montana stage race and billed it as the unofficial world championship of climbing. In 1985, battling the altitude and humidity, American Andy Hampsten put in a amazing climbing performance, beating the conditions and competition to come away with the race victory and continuing a series of major American climbing exploits against the best riders in the world.

The American Advance

By 1986 the great French rider, Bernard Hinault, had won five Tours de France and was the dominant rider of his generation. After publicly stating that he would support Greg Lemond in the 1986 TdF, Hinault held a one minute lead on his young teammate in that year's race entering the Pyrenees Mountains. The next day Hinault attacked, and Lemond, very frustrated in the domestique role, could not follow, giving up almost another five minutes by the end of the stage. The following day started as a repeat of the previous one as Hinault again went to the front. On the last climb of the day the race leaders, including Hinault and Lemond, were in the lead group. Multiple attacks were launched and this time Lemond did not hold back. With help from teammate Andy Hampsten, Lemond broke away early on the climb and, pulling away from Hampsten, crushed the stage, picking up almost all of the time he had lost to Hinault the day before. Showing he was now the best rider in the world, Lemond went on to win the Tour, becoming the first American to do so.

Italy Finally Falls

The Giro d'Italia is Italy's grand cycling tour. With a storied history it is the second most difficult race in the world to win. Italy has perhaps the toughest road climbs in Europe but if not, it certainly has more difficult climbs to include in its stages compared to the other major tours, and they are often put to good use. In 1988, Andy Hampsten was riding well as the Giro began. After a solid finish in the opening stage time trial the American hung around until the hills, gradually moving up in general classification. On Stage 12, the first with a hill finish, Hampsten won and put himself very close to the overall lead. The Giro was in the mountains at this point and Stage 14 would be a turning point. The big climb on that stage was up Gavia Pass, a very high, steep and difficult hill. In a pouring rain the peloton stayed together until the base of the Gavia and at that point no one knew what awaited up above on its cruel slopes. As the riders attacked the hill the rain turned to sleet and then to snow near the top. Hampsten stayed with the lead group as riders were shredded around him by the hill and the weather, many abandoning the stage. Hampsten, familiar with the conditions from his training days in Colorado, gritted his teeth and kept pumping the pedals, eventually finishing second in the stage but taking the overall race lead and putting all but one rider minutes behind him in the general classification. He survived multiple attacks over the last week of the race and then won the mountain time trial at the end to cruise to victory, becoming the first and only American to win the Giro d'Italia.

To Descend One Must Climb

After Greg Lemond's dominating win in the 1986 Tour de France the terrible story of his hunting accident is well known, an event that kept him off the bike and on the sidelines for nearly two years. Who knows what his already solid legacy may have been had he been healthy (and had he not had to endure several TdFs as a domestique to the great Bernard Hinault). With his performance capacity obviously diminished after the accident, he put on an amazing time trialing exhibition to win the 1989 Tour, performing well but not superbly in the mountains. In the 1990 TdF the same circumstances were present; Lemond was fit and able but still not quite his old self. The days of his physical domination over, he would need to win races not by brawn but by brains and will. Heading into the key stage in the Pyrenees just over halfway through the race, Lemond found himself behind Italy's Claudio Chiappucci by almost three minutes. As the mountain stages were almost over it was now or never if an assault on a third TdF was to be undertaken. The stage contained three giant climbs lined up over the last half of the route. Chiappucci attacked right at the base of the first climb and flew away, opening a big lead at the summit and increasing it, halfway up the next climb, the mighty Tourmalet, to over three minutes for the stage and almost six minutes overall. Realizing that a critical point had been reached, Lemond launched a severe attack up the Tourmalet, halving the gap to Chiappucci by the summit. The descent of the Tourmalet is a long one, twisting down through very dangerous turns. Always known as a good bike handler, Lemond came down the Tourmalet like a bat out of hell and by the bottom had caught Chiappucci! Making up a gap of one and a half minutes on a descent over another top professional bike rider is an amazing feat, and highlights the importance of descending in mountain stages. However, while catching the stage leader was a heroic effort there were still over eight miles of climbing yet to come before the finish and Chiapucci still had a large overall race lead. The small leading group headed up the final hill and stayed together over much of the final climb. With two miles remaining to the summit however another rider in the group attacked and Lemond went with him, dropping Chiappucci. The smaller group drove hard to the finish, dropping all but two riders by the end (Lemond and future five time TdF winner Miguel Indurain). By the finish Lemond had picked up almost three minutes on the race leader, cutting the overall lead to five seconds, a margin he could easily pick up during the last time trial stage before the race finish in Paris. Going on to win his third TdF, Lemond won the race on the slopes of the Pyrenees with an amazing climbing performance.

The Alp

First used in the Tour de France in 1952, L'Alpe d'Huez, with its multiple, numbered switchbacks, has become one of the most recognizable climbs in the world. Often used as a stage finish, the climb may be the true symbol of the Tour as decisive moments are often played out on its slopes. Almost mythic in stature, all of cycling's greats have done battle there and winning a stage atop the legendary Alp has become one of the most revered accomplishments in cycling. While certainly performing well at the highest level of the sport, Andy Hampsten came to the 1992 TdF without a top level result that matched the climbing exploits that led to his 1988 win in the Giro d'Italia. The Alps that year contained perhaps the most difficult stage of the race, containing four major climbs and ending on top of L'Alpe d'Huez. Feeling well that day, something stirred in Hampsten as he ascended the third climb of the day. Breaking away in a small group, they opened a gap on the field and descended toward L'Alpe. By the base of the climb the group had a four minute lead on everyone else. By the first of many hairpin turns Hampsten was alone. Using an increasingly larger gear he charged up the hill through the huge crowds, gradually pulling away and winning the stage. By conquering the legendary climb he joined cycling's legends on perhaps its most prized summit.

Mount Washington Falls

Mount Washington in New Hampshire may be the toughest climb in the world, with an average grade of

Scenery along the way to Independence Pass

Descending awaits west of Boulder

almost 12% and portions of the route unpaved. The climb is a brutal one with no flats or descents to catch your breath and riders must often battle cold temperatures and howling winds. An annual hill climb race has been held on its slopes for many years, with the record for the climb having been set way back in 1980. The record stood for seventeen years until a young professional rider, Tyler Hamilton, arrived in 1997 and crushed the competition, lowering the record by almost six minutes in the process, a huge percentage decrease. The record has been lowered subsequently by small margins but Hamilton set the stage and drew attention, as well as some of the world's top riders, to what now may be the most coveted prize in American cycling climbing.

Ventoux

Often used in stage races, Mont Ventoux is a beast of a climb, perhaps the most difficult in France. Soon after the climb begins the trees and most vegetation disappear and riders are left stuck in a barren, parched moonscape that seems to sap the energy of anyone that moves through it. Often used in major European races such as the Dauphine Libere, a major stage race held the month before the Tour de France, Mont Ventoux is a climb that is feared by all riders. Many use the Dauphine as preparation for the Tour so Ventoux has been graced by all of cycling's greats through the years with many a heroic battle having been fought on its slopes, including the death of pro Tom Simpson in 1967 and a memorable duel between Lance Armstrong and Marco Pantani in the 2000 Tour de France. In fact the mountain became Armstrong's nemesis as he failed to win a race that ended on its slopes. The record for the climb had been set way back in 1955 by the great Charley Gaul, a TdF and Giro d'Italia winner with the nickname 'the angel of the mountains'. In 1999 the Dauphine included a time trial up Ventoux for Stage 3. As horrible as the mountain is within the peloton, it is even worse during a time trial. All alone against the hill, riders must dig deep and find an unaided way to the top. American Jonathan Vaughters came to the starting gate that day feeling pretty good. A very successful pro, he entered the stage close to the overall lead and felt a big move on Ventoux could be the difference between winning and losing the race. Vaughters attacked the hill from the beginning, gradually putting time on his opponents at each time check and won the stage, breaking the 44-year-old record for the climb.

A New Beginning

Many questions surrounded Lance Armstrong when the 1999 Tour de France began, including his ability to compete for one, having come back to the sport after a vicious battle with cancer (although that question had been answered with some success in pre Tour races). A second question was his ability to climb. A big time trial win early in the race had given him the overall lead as the peloton headed into the Alps. Skeptics were noting however that it was very unlikely that the American could continue his success into the big mountains of the tour. Never a great climber before his illness surely he would succumb once the roads tilted upward. The ninth stage of that year's race was a brutal one. It included six major climbs including the beyond category Galibier in France and Sestrieres in Italy, hallowed ground where all of cycling's greats had battled over the years. To make things worse the weather was poor that day so that the upper altitudes were shrouded in cold and wet weather. In the small lead group at the base of the last climb of the day were many of the best climbers in the race. As they ascended, several fell away so that only four remained. With three miles to go Armstrong attacked, opening a small gap. As the gap grew he poured it on in such a way that no one could respond, pulling away to win the stage by thirty-one seconds and widening his race lead over the top contenders to an almost insurmountable margin. Having dropped almost fifteen pounds and recovered his power since his illness, Armstrong had turned himself into a climbing machine. If there was any doubt regarding his abilities to climb the biggest mountains it was now gone as he went on to win his first TdF.

It Was No Fluke

Before the 2000 Tour de France many cycling pundits felt that Lance Armstrong's 1999 Tour win was a fluke of sorts. With several of the best riders absent that year they reasoned, he would be unlikely to repeat as champion in 2000 when the field included all of the top contenders. As the 2000 event got underway Lance soon found himself down by a wide margin in the overall classification and with a small lead over those considered his strongest competition. A few days later the Tour entered the mountains for the first time and with that a chance for riders to make a big move on the leader board. As the last climb of the day got underway in cold and rainy conditions up the

Steep climbing on Mount Evans

The top of scenic Loveland Pass

Hautacam, a tough climb in the Pyrenees Mountains, the leading group contained many race contenders with several of them out ahead due to an early breakaway. Soon the group was attacked by 1998 Tour winner Marco Pantani, one of those absent from the 1999 Tour. Armstrong quickly closed the gap, in the process dropping several, among them Jan Ullrich, the 1997 TdF winner and another rider absent in 1999. Even on a very strong day it is a difficult thing for a cyclist to push an attack early on a climb. It is best to wait to see what shakes out as the finish line gets closer. An early attack is considered either foolish bravado or a heroic act depending upon the outcome. However, on that day Armstrong's instincts proved the better of conventional cycling wisdom. Once he had caught and passed Pantani he actually picked up the tempo and pulled away. The rest of the group could not respond and disappeared backward as Lance flew up the mountain. Continuing to charge to the finish line in a steady rain Armstrong caught all but one of the early breakaway riders. But more importantly he had put serious time on all of the top contenders, picking up anywhere from three to five minutes on each. While there was much more riding to be done, the Tour was essentially over and Armstrong had answered one more question.

Changing of the Guard Delayed

Jeannie Longo, an eleven time world champion, came to New Hampshire from France in 2000 looking for a different kind of challenge. Up against the defending women's champion, 18-year-old Genevieve Jeansson of Canada, and perhaps the hardest climb on earth, Mount Washington, Longo knew that she had her work cut out for her during the annual hillclimb race up its slopes. As the race begun, Jeansson took a forty second lead at the two mile mark as the climb headed into its steepest miles. Longo's experience began to show however as she gradually picked up the pace, catching Jeansson at four miles and opening a gap. Jeansson fought back and attacked but she could not quite close to the leader. Longo pulled away, opening a two minute lead and, in what is one of the most amazing climbing performances of all time, at forty-one years of age, won the race, passing all but the two top men and setting the women's record for the hill in the process.

The Look

In the 2001 Tour de France Lance Armstrong, having won the previous two Tours, was in a battle with German rider Jan Ullrich, a former Tour winner and his biggest threat to another victory, as the race entered the first mountain stage. The stage contained three beyond category climbs, ending on the top of the third, the famous L'Alpe d'Huez. Over the first two monster climbs, the Col de la Madeleine and the Col du Glandon, Armstrong struggled just to stay at the back of the lead group. At the beginning of the climb up L'Alpe, Ullrich and several teammates led the way. Suddenly Armstrong shot to the front, pulled there by his teammate Jose Luis Rubiero. As Rubiero pulled off and with Ullrich on his wheel, Armstrong came out of the saddle, and in a moment that has become one of the greatest in cycling history, turned to look back at his competition for a long moment, and accelerated away. Ullrich and the rest of the field had no response and

Armstrong won the stage, picking up two minutes on his main rival on the way to his third Tour victory and further cementing his place in the folklore of cycling history.

Redemption

Perhaps driven by her loss to Jeannie Longo of France two years before, Canadian Genevieve Jeansson came to Mount Washington in 2002 with something to prove. The annual hillclimb race up its slopes is perhaps the most brutal on earth but no doubt having lost the event to someone more than twice her age in 2000 must have been incentive enough to draw her back again. She exploded up the hill right from the start, putting time on all of her competition. The road up Mount Washington never wavers and neither did Jeansson that day as she continued her torrid pace all the way to the top, winning the race by a margin of over ten minutes and breaking the hillclimb record previously held by Longo by over four minutes. Only two male riders finished ahead of her as she set a standard that has not since been approached and may be difficult to surpass.

The 'Off' Year

2003 is a year that Lance Armstrong and cycling fans will not forget. It was the year that almost wasn't; the year that Lance could be beaten. Struggling somewhat through the first half of the race Armstrong found himself with a slim lead as the first individual time trial approached. His lead due mostly to a winning team time trial performance, even Armstrong himself knew that something wasn't quite right that year. His pulls were not quite as they had been in years past and his race leading margin showed it. In the time trial Armstrong suffered, whether from mistakes or lack of preparation, and German Jan Ullrich, Lance's chief rival and in second place overall, did what had not been done in a major tour since 1996 as he put hurt and time on the Texas rider and trimmed his slim overall race lead to seconds. Armstrong looked like a beaten man and with only a fifteen second lead most believed that this was the time that he would finally fall as the tour headed into the Pyrenees and the toughest stage of the tour. Containing a category 1 and two beyond category climbs this would be the last chance for the race contenders to take time out of one another before the final time trial. After multiple attacks the second to last climb of the day, the Tourmalet, was descended. At the bottom, the lead group (with one rider several minutes ahead) was a strong one as it started up the Luz-Ardiden to finish the stage. As the group began the brutal climb among tightly packed fans along the route, Armstrong's handle bar caught an obstruction among the spectators, throwing him hard to the ground. Once back up and struggling to restart, his foot detached from his pedal, causing another delay. The lead riders, having moved ahead, slowed in order for the Texan to get back into the climb but much momentum had been lost. Almost immediately after the excitement, the group reformed and Spanish rider Iban Mayo attacked, opening a small gap. After over 100 miles of hard riding and having to remount after hitting the pavement, just finishing the stage would have been considered a victory. Following an attack at that point would seem to be impossible. However, Armstrong immediately jumped the gap to Mayo and, sensing an opportunity, attacked himself. No one else could keep his wheel as he pulled away. Maintaining a brutal pace on the steep and famous climb he soon shredded all of the cyclist behind him, including his main rival, Jan Ullrich.

Putting his game face on, Armstrong continued to hammer up the hill, soon catching the lead rider and heading for the finish. Sweat pouring off of him, he knew every second counted in this very close race. Picking up a time bonus as he won the stage, Armstrong showed who was still the boss in 2003 as he gained time on all of his rivals, eventually securing his fifth Tour de France victory. It was said that this was what Henry Desgrange, the Tour founder, wanted when he added big hills to the race route; suffering and victory no matter what the cost!

Mountain Domination

The 2004 Tour de France held great pressure for Lance Armstrong as he tried to become the first six-time winner of the storied event. While certainly dominant in mountain stages in the past it was as if he had made a conscious decision in 2004 to waste no opportunity as he completed the three week race. When the mountain stages appeared, the other riders certainly knew that the Texan was there to win. As the following accounts attest, Lance was giving away nothing that year and documents one of the most dominating periods of mountain riding ever witnessed.

The top of Magnolia Road

The steep start up Flagstaff Mountain

Stage 12

As the 2004 Tour de France finally got to the real mountains (Pyrennes) Armstrong was over five minutes down in the general classification. After a flat first half the stage ended with two tough climbs. In a bunch near the lead at the base of the last climb, La Mongie, what was left of Armstrong's U.S. Postal team pulled the train, gradually wearing out the rest of the group. After his teammates dropped off, Lance responded to an attack, pulled even and then launched an attack himself. Only a few riders are able to stay with him as he headed for the finish. Attacking again Armstrong ended up on the wheel of the only one ahead of him, Italian Ivan Basso. The two pulled away and while certainly looking like he could have taken the stage win, Armstrong settled for second, picking up valuable time on everyone else. If it was a gift, it was certainly the last one of 2004.

Stage 13

The thirteenth stage of the 2004 TdF was the first true mountain stage of the race. After topping six climbs the U.S. Postal team train had reduced the peloton almost to ruins as only a small group was still in contention halfway through the final climb up the beyond category Plateau de Beille. Once the last of his teammates dropped off, the two strongest climbers in the 2004 race were once again going head to head. Working together this time, both Ivan Basso and Armstrong take turns leading up the severe, unrelenting slope through the mass of fans lining the roadway. Higher and higher they climbed through the human sea, each looking for the finish. With under a mile to go Armstrong zipped up his jersey; he would go for it today! With the line in site the Texan accelerated around Basso for the win.

Stage 15

After a transition ride toward the Alps for Stage 14, the peloton headed into the big mountains for Stage 15. While not containing any giant hills the route was packed with challenging climbs. At the base of the last climb the leading group is full of the usual suspects, including of course, Armstrong. The powerful group relentlessly moved up the hill, shredding riders along the way. As the finish line approached, four strong riders were left, those who would make up four of the top five places in the general classification at day's end. Ivan Basso made the first move but Armstrong, timing his attack to perfection, swung under the Italian around a corner to take the stage win, picking up the yellow jersey as the tour leader for the first time in the race.

Stage 16

The climb up L'Alpe d'Huez in the Alps is one of most difficult used in the Tour de France. In the 2004 version, one of the time trial stages was a battle up its slopes. In time trials, riders are all alone, forced to set tempo by themselves, as they start two minutes apart with their starting time determined by their place in the general classification (the last place rider goes first, the first place rider goes last..). Huge crowds lined the route, the largest of the race so far. Over the early phase of the ride Armstrong rode conservatively, and was in ninth place at the first time check. Picking up the pace in the middle of the race, Lance started to make up time, spinning his high cadence style up the slope. Soon another rider appeared in front of him, a target to acquire. It was Basso, his nemesis over the last week, who was getting caught, despite having started a full two minutes ahead! Armstrong pulled even and, not even glancing at his rival, accelerated around a corner and disappeared up the road. His face grim with determination, he continued to put time on every rider. As he crossed the finish line the stage, and the Tour, were all but over. Battling a mass of fans that parted only at the last minute as the riders passed, throwing water, encouragement, epithets and worse, Armstrong put in another amazing climbing performance, winning the stage and picking up additional minutes on all his rivals as he moved toward his record setting sixth TdF win. As Lance said afterwards, "I wanted it bad. I wanted it for the history on the mountain…"

Stage 17

With the GC lead and multiple stage wins at this point, conventional wisdom might have been to take it easy on the last mountain stage; to take no chances and cruise into Paris for the trophy. However, this was 2004 and something was in the air. A very tough day led over three category 1 and one beyond category climbs. The usual scenario played out as a strong group of five riders, including Armstrong, led over the top of the last big climb of the day. After a descent, the finishing stretch was rolling terrain with a slightly uphill finish. Armstrong's teammate, Floyd Landis, was in the lead group, and looking to pick up a stage win. With less than two kilometers to go Landis

Elevation at the top of Big Thompson Canyon

Scenery along Route 7 near Lyons

attacked but everyone went with him and soon he was reeled in. At the one kilometer to go mark the German rider Andreas Kloden suddenly took off from the back of the pack, surprising everyone and opening a big gap. It appeared the stage was his. As he saw Landis's hopes of winning fading away, Armstrong came out of the saddle and began to sprint. Pulling away from the others he amazingly closed the gap to Kloden in a flash and pulled past the German at the line, winning his third stage in a row. Winning four of five mountain stages (and finishing second in the fifth) Armstrong's performance in the 2004 TdF was one of the most dominating climbing exhibitions ever seen.

Top of the World

As previously mentioned, Mount Evans in Colorado is one of the most difficult climbs in the U.S. With the road soaring to over 14,000 feet, much of its difficulty is due to altitude. The annual race up its slopes always draws many top climbers but by 2004 it had been twelve years since the course record had been assaulted. With snow having fallen the previous day and in cold and foggy conditions, American Tom Danielson put in a spectacular performance as he won the race by an unheard of 8 minutes and 40 seconds, chopping 4 minutes and 10 seconds off of the record. Having been training extensively at altitude and in mid-season form Danielson, one of the best climbers in the world (the current record holder on Mount Washington as of 2006 and multiple other climbs), raised the bar on Mount Evans and set a standard that may be difficult to surpass for some time to come.

The Lieutenant Strikes

Longtime faithful lieutenant to Lance Armstrong but a highly skilled rider in his own right, George Hincapie had never won a Tour de France stage despite numerous one day race wins. Stage 15 of the 2005 TdF was the most difficult of the race, containing four category 1 climbs and one beyond category climb to finish the stage. Getting into a breakaway early, Hincapie fought off many attacks as the stage progressed. Finally, on the last climb of the day, the Pla-d'Adet, Hincapie and Oscar Pereiro, who had done much of the leg work in the breakaway, pulled away from what was left of the leading group as the finish line approached. Marking Pereiro up the cruel steeps, Hincapie stayed behind while looking for the finish line. With 200 hundred meters to go he swung around the Spanish rider who had no response and charged to the hilltop win, becoming one of only a handful of Americans to win a major tour mountain stage.

A Tradition Continues

The 2006 Tour de France was considered wide open after the great one, Lance Armstrong, retired after his 7th straight win. American Floyd Landis came into that year's race well prepared. Having won several prestigious titles that year, he was poised to take over where Lance had left off. Leading the race as it headed into the Alps, Landis bonked on stage 16, losing his lead and much of his dignity in the process. Stage 17, he knew, might be his last chance at ever winning the Tour. It was a tough stage, with multiple difficult climbs along its route. Attacking early, the other riders sat back, thinking a move at this point was suicide. However, Landis knew just was he was doing. He quickly overtook an earlier breakaway group and continued hammering up the hills. Soon he was up by over nine minutes. What was left of the peloton finally woke up and began chasing in earnest. On the final climb of day, the beyond category Col de Joux Plane, Landis blew his last stage challenger off of his wheel and had a five minute lead at the summit. He then picked up an incredible additional 30 seconds on the field during the descent. Gaining over seven minutes on the overall leader that day, he went on to eventually win the TdF. Having attacked for over 80 miles through mountainous terrain, Landis's ride that day was one of the greatest in Tour history.

A rider on upper Mount Evans

Map

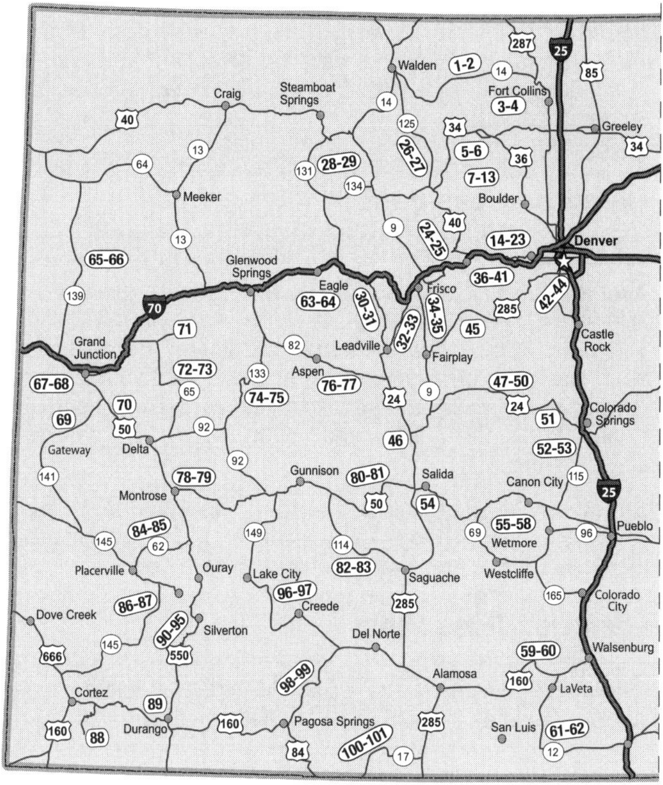

KEY

(1-2) = Climb location

 # corresponds to Table of Contents listing.

Northeast Colorado

Northeast Colorado is defined as the area from Route 40/131 (Steamboat Springs) east to Interstate 25 and north of Interstate 70. It includes Boulder and part of the Denver metro area.

Cameron Pass East

Total elevation - 2,239 ft	**Length - 12.1 miles**
Average Grade - 3.5% (6%)	**Rating - 0.95 (cat 2)**

This climb is a shallow ascent up to Cameron Pass (Route 14). The ride is pleasant as the road has small shoulders but not a lot of traffic. If you would like to ride the entire route from Route 287 it is ~57 miles and ~5000 feet of very shallow elevation gain.

Directions - In Fort Collins head north on Route 287 for a short distance to Route 14. Head west on 14 for ~45 miles to the Tunnel Picnic Area on the left (dirt road) to begin.

Cameron Pass West

Total elevation - 1,265 ft	**Length - 7.9 miles**
Average Grade - 3.0% (5%)	**Rating - 0.46 (cat 3)**

The west side of Cameron Pass is also a pleasant ascent but a bit shorter.

Directions - In Walden head east on Route 14 for ~22 miles to Gould where the climb begins by continuing east on 14.

Rist Canyon East

Total elevation - 2,813 ft	Length - 10.5 miles
Average Grade - 5.1% (13%)	Rating - 1.64 (cat 1)

The east side of Rist Canyon is a solid climb to altitude northwest of Fort Collins. Shallow to start you soon enter a scenic canyon and the road gets twisty. The grade is more variable here and there is a flat section and a descent. You break out of the canyon toward the top and the last 0.5 miles are along double digit grade so the summit is a welcome site.

Directions - In Fort Collins head north on Route 287 to 54G on the left (if you reach Route 14 you missed the turn). Head down 54G for a short distance and Rist Canyon Road will appear on the right. Travel Rist Canyon Road through tiny Bellvue. As you leave town you cross Route 25 where the listed climb begins.

Rist Canyon West

Total elevation - 677 ft	Length - 1.4 miles
Average Grade - 9.2% (12%)	Rating - 0.69 (cat 2)

The west side of Rist Canyon is a short and steep ascent. The grade is shallow to start but the last mile is one of the steepest in Colorado. It is also a very quick descent.

Directions - In Fort Collins head west on Route 38 to Masonville. Once there head north on Route 27 for 14.5 rolling (and at times steep) miles to Rist Canyon Road on the right where the climb begins.

Trail Ridge East

Total elevation - 4,661 ft	**Length - 18.2 miles**
Average Grade - 4.8% (7%)	**Rating - 2.83 (hors/cat 1)**

One of the most difficult climbs in Colorado, the east side of Trail Ridge northwest of Denver is a very spectacular ascent into Rocky Mountain National Park. Quite shallow to start, after several miles you pass through the NP entrance gate ($5 for bikes). Mountain meadows dominate the lower portion and you soon begin to switchback a bit up the mountain. The grade is fairly steady and never steep as the road soon begins to hug the ridge in places through the middle of the ascent. Near the top the setting is tundra-like with great mountain views as you summit at Trail Ridge (12,183 ft), one of the highest passes in the United States. There is a false flat just before the true summit. This road keeps you above treeline for a greater distance than any other in the state except for mighty Mount Evans. It is a long and shallow hill but don't underestimate the elevation attained on this climb. Due to its elevation it has a pretty short window to ride and does carry a lot of traffic at times so ride early in the day if possible (closed in winter - Rocky Mountain National Park 970 586-1206). The road is never closed to bikes however so one way to beat the traffic is to ride it in the fall right after closure. Due to its sharp turns and exposure in places (along with its scenery) Trail Ridge East is a challenging descent as well.

Directions - The climb begins at the western edge of Estes Park, CO at the last traffic light before leaving town on Route 36. Head up Route 36 to begin.

Near the top of the west side of Trail Ridge

Early views toward Cottonwood Pass

Trail Ridge West

Total elevation - 3,814 ft **Length - 26.5 miles**
Average Grade - 2.7% (6%) **Rating - 1.30 (cat 2)**

One of the most scenic climbs in the US, the west side of Trail Ridge is long and somewhat isolated. It is over shallow grade over its entire length but the elevation may make you work for its top. The road is quite narrow and carries some traffic at times. Near the top you break out of the trees for spectacular views before ending at over 12,000 feet.

Directions - At the north end of Grand Lake, CO on Route 34 the climb begins by heading north on Route 34 toward the National Park.

Big Thompson Canyon

Total elevation - 2,196 ft **Length - 17.4 miles**
Average Grade - 2.4% (6%) **Rating - 0.57 (cat 2)**

The ascent of Big Thompson Canyon (Route 34 East) is a shallow climb to Estes Park along a busy road. There is good scenery in Big Thompson Canyon along most of the route but traffic makes this one difficult. The climb ends at Mall Road on the left just as you enter Estes Park.

Directions - In Loveland head west on Route 34. Once you pass Route 27 on the right the Dam Store appears in another 2.4 miles (right) where the listed climb begins by continuing west on Route 34.

36 East

Total elevation - 2,678 ft **Length - 16.0 miles**

Average Grade - 3.2% (7%) **Rating - 0.95 (cat 2)**

Another route to Estes Park and Rocky Mountain National Park, the east side of Route 36 is a long climb over mostly shallow grade and carries quite a bit of traffic at times. There is a descent about halfway up and the hill ends at an unmarked but obvious top (Pole Hill Road on the right).

Directions - In Lyons at the junction of Routes 7 and 36 head west on 36 (to the city limits) for 0.6 miles to begin the listed climb.

7 East

Total elevation - 2,749 ft **Length - 13.8 miles**

Average Grade - 3.8% (8%) **Rating - 1.16 (cat 2)**

A less travelled road than Route 36, the east side of Route 7 is shallow overall but is scenic over much of its route and carries much less traffic than Route 36. There is a very tight section at one point along increased grade. Near the top you pass Route 72 on the left and the listed climb peaks in another 0.5 miles (unmarked).

Directions - In Lyons at the junction of Routes 7 and 36 head west on Route 7 for one mile to begin the climb at the end of a descent.

Lefthand Canyon/Ward Road

Total elevation - 3,361ft	**Length - 14.4 miles**
Average Grade - 4.4% (12%)	**Rating - 1.77 (cat 1)**

Tame to start, this climb will bite you in its upper sections. From the parking area head up Lefthand Canyon over a moderate grade and some twisty turns. At mile 2.7 turn left on Ward Road (straight for Super James). Ward Road gradually gets steeper as you gain altitude. The last two miles are steeper (this section is broken in two by a small village) and you reach the top through a steep switchback (max grade) as the climb ends at the Peak to Peak Highway at over 9,000 feet.

Directions - From Route 36 just north of Boulder head west on Lefthand Canyon Road for 2.5 miles (Old Stage Road on left) where the climb begins.

Super James

Total elevation - 2,617 ft	**Length - 9.5 miles**
Average Grade - 5.2% (11%)	**Rating - 1.55 (cat 1)**

This climb shares its start and first few miles with the previous ascent (Lefthand Canyon). At Ward Road keep straight toward Jamestown along increasing grade. The road here is tight through sweeping turns. Once past town the grade increases as the last 3 miles are the most difficult (~8% avg grade) and the listed climb ends at Sparn Road on the left.

Directions - See previous climb.

Double digit grade on upper Ward Road

Scenery on Super James

Lee Hill/Deer Trail Road

Total elevation - 2,077 ft	**Length - 6.0 miles**
Average Grade - 6.6% (16%)	**Rating - 1.72 (cat 1)**

A steep ascent, Lee Hill Road quickly leaves Boulder and begins climbing. Keep left on Lee Hill at its junction with Old Stage Road and receive double digit grade. Soon views appear and a short descent. Soon after climbing resumes, turn left on Deer Trail Road (straight to descend to Lefthand Canyon). This upper section is variable and contains double digit grade and the max grade of the ascent. The climb ends at Mine Lane (dirt).

Directions - In Boulder head west on Lee Hill Drive from Broadway to 4th Street (on the left) where the listed climb begins.

Sunshine Canyon

Total elevation - 1,242 ft	**Length - 3.0 miles**
Average Grade - 7.8% (12%)	**Rating - 1.05 (cat 2)**

Sunshine Canyon is another challenging ascent just west of Boulder. You begin over shallow grade which gradually increases. A switchback announces more serious climbing and the listed hill ends after 3 miles. The road continues for another 2.6 miles before turning to dirt but real climbing has ended. Stats for the full pavement ride are 5.6 miles at 5.8% avg grade.

Directions - In Boulder head west on Mapleton from Broadway. The listed climb begins just beyond the community hospital at Greenrock Drive on the left.

Four Mile Canyon

Total elevation - 1,210 ft	**Length - 5.6 miles**
Average Grade - 4.1% (8%)	**Rating - 0.52 (cat 3)**

Four Mile Canyon is a pleasant ascent just west of Boulder and close to steeper climbing. The road is tight and the grade moderate (there is a half mile descent/flat along the way) until you reach a small community. At that point the grade increases and the road turns to dirt at mile 5.6.

Directions - In Boulder head west on Canyon for several miles and Four Mile Canyon Road will appear on the right where the listed climb begins.

Boulder Canyon

Total elevation - 2,623 ft	**Length - 13.3 miles**
Average Grade - 3.7% (10%)	**Rating - 1.13 (cat 2)**

Boulder Canyon is a long and moderate grade climb in a narrow canyon that begins in Boulder and takes you to the Peak to Peak Highway and other rides. The grade is very shallow to start and there is traffic most days. Toward the middle of the ascent more stout grade arrives. The grade eases again near the top and the listed climb ends at the dam and lake just before you reach the Peak to Peak Highway.

Directions - In Boulder head west on Canyon (Route 119) from Broadway for several miles to begin the listed climb at Arapahoe Avenue on the left.

Sugarloaf Road

Total elevation - 1,960 ft	**Length - 4.8 miles**
Average Grade - 7.7% (12%)	**Rating - 1.70 (cat 1)**

This hill starts out steep along a very tight, twisty road with good views before the canyon closes in. The grade moderates and there is a small descent along this stretch. After 2.1 miles the grade increases to double digit in places and continues to be challenging all the way to pavement end.

Directions - In Boulder head west on Canyon for several miles and Sugarloaf will be on the right (just beyond Magnolia Road).

Magnolia Road

Total elevation - 2,170 ft	**Length - 4.5 miles**
Average Grade - 9.1% (17%)	**Rating - 2.40 (cat 1)**

Magnolia Road is one of the steepest climbs in CO. Be ready early on as the route is severe immediately through tight turns. The first mile is the steepest and through several big switchbacks. You encounter several small descents in the middle of the climb which knock down the average grade of this monster. There are two more big switchbacks over the 2nd half with grade in their inner corners of 25%. Near the top the slope finally eases and the climb ends where the road turns to dirt.

Directions - From Broadway and Canyon Road in Boulder head west on Canyon for ~5 miles to Magnolia (left) to begin the climb.

The start of steep Magnolia Road

Exposure on Sugarloaf Road

Flagstaff Road

Total elevation - 1,968 ft **Length - 4.6 miles**
Average Grade - 8.1% (14%) **Rating - 1.77 (cat 1)**

Flagstaff Road is a solid climb just southeast of Boulder. You encounter double digit grade almost immediately and the first mile is difficult. Several big switchbacks carry you to its unmarked top. There is a double digit grade mile from Realization Point but almost the entire route is stout. It is a tough descent due to its steep grade and tight turns. At times the road can carry a bit of traffic as well.

Directions - In Boulder from Broadway head west on Baseline. Travel Baseline 1.5 miles west and the listed climb begins at Gregory Canyon Trailhead (left).

NCAR

Total elevation - 683 ft **Length - 2.5 miles**
Average Grade - 5.2% (9%) **Rating - 0.37 (cat 3)**

NCAR (National Center for Atmospheric Research) is a short and stout climb close to Boulder. The first stretch is moderate but once you leave a neighborhood the grade and view increases and the climb ends at the research center on top. It is a fast descent as well.

Directions - Heading south on Broadway from Boulder turn right (west) on Table Mesa Drive where the climb begins.

A rider descends Flagstaff Mountain

Views from NCAR near Boulder

Coal Creek Canyon

Total elevation - 2,009 ft	**Length - 8.4 miles**
Average Grade - 4.5% (7%)	**Rating - 1.04 (cat 2)**

The east side of Coal Creek Canyon (Route 72) is a somewhat isolated climb northwest of Golden. A moderate grade greets you as the canyon closes in. Soon the road gets very tight and twisty and at mile 4.8 the village of Coal Creek appears. The climbing continues but the grade is never steep on this one and the climb ends in Wondervu at an obvious top.

Directions - In Golden head north on Route 93 toward Boulder. At the junction with Route 72 head west for 2.5 miles to the railroad bridge across the mouth of Coal Creek Canyon to begin the listed climb.

Golden Gate Canyon

Total elevation - 2,739 ft	**Length - 11.3 miles**
Average Grade - 4.6% (11%)	**Rating - 1.47 (cat 1/2)**

Golden Gate Canyon parallels the previous climb and is a bit steeper overall. The 2nd half is more challenging (mile near the top is just under 10%) and the listed climb ends at Bear Paw Road on the left. The road from that point to Peak to Peak Highway continues to climb but intermittently.

Directions - In Golden, CO head north on Route 93 for a short distance to Golden Gate Canyon Road (Route 46) on the left to begin the climb.

A rider ascends Golden Gate Canyon near Denver

Views from Lookout Mountain

Lookout Mountain Road

Total elevation - 1,438 ft	**Length - 5.1 miles**
Average Grade - 5.3% (7%)	**Rating - 0.84 (cat 2)**

Lookout Mountain Road is an area icon and is one of the closest real climbs to Denver so it sees a lot of riders in good weather. Never steep, the route is very scenic as it twists up the mountain through some tight switchbacks and exposure in places but that also means good views. Towards the end the grade eases and the listed climb ends just before the road to the Buffalo Bill Museum and grave (post). Pillar to post stats are 4.7 miles at 5.1%.

Directions - In Golden go to the intersection of Route 6 and 19th Street where the listed climb begins by heading west on 19th. The pillars are just up the road from that junction.

119

Total elevation – 2,426 ft	**Length - 12.6 miles**
Average Grade - 3.6% (8%)	**Rating - 1.03 (cat 2)**

Route 119 is a long and shallow climb through Blackhawk and the southern end of the Peak to Peak Highway. After ~ 6 miles you enter busy Blackhawk and find 4 lanes. Beyond town the number of lanes and traffic decrease and the best climbing arrives. The ascent ends at the junction with Route 46 (right).

Directions - The listed climb begins at the junction of Routes 119 and 6 by heading north on 119 (toward Blackhawk).

Berthoud Pass North

Total elevation - 2,197 ft **Length - 10.2 miles**

Average Grade - 4.1% (6%) **Rating - 1.10 (cat 2)**

The north side of Berthoud Pass is another classic alpine climb just south of Winterpark. Never steep, the climb can work you a bit due to its length and altitude attained. The route is twisty in spots and a wide road and steady grade makes for a pleasant ride most days. The top is signed and affords views of some snow capped peaks.

Directions - In Winterpark on Route 40 head south to the last stoplight in town (Winterpark resort) to begin this climb.

Berthoud Pass South

Total elevation - 2,524 ft **Length - 11.2 miles**

Average Grade - 4.2% (6%) **Rating - 1.32 (cat 1/2)**

The south side of Berthoud Pass is a steady grade ascent to high altitude. Never steep, the road sweeps through long, multiple switchbacks on its way to the top. There is good scenery along the way and at the summit. It is a fun and somewhat technical descent as well as you can gain speed on the long switchbacks and then must negotiate multiple hairpin turns.

Directions - On Route 40 in Empire, CO head west for a short distance to the Arapahoe National Forest sign (right) to begin the listed climb.

Willow Creek Pass North

Total elevation - 1,063 ft | **Length - 9.8 miles**

Average Grade - 2.1% (5%) | **Rating - 0.26 (cat 3)**

The north side of Willow Creek Pass is a shallow ascent to moderate altitude. Very shallow to start, the last few miles are a bit steeper and quite scenic but none of this route will test you and the climb tops out at 9,683 feet.

Directions - From Walden, CO on Route 125 head south for ~22 miles to the very small town of Rand to begin the listed climb by continuing south on 125.

Willow Creek Pass South

Total elevation - 1,832 ft | **Length - 21.7 miles**

Average Grade - 1.7% (5%) | **Rating - 0.34 (cat 3)**

The south side of Willow Creek Pass is a long and shallow climb west of Rocky Mountain National Park. There is a descent several miles in and then climbing resumes. Never steep, it is a pleasant ride with the last few miles being a bit steeper. The south side of Willow Creek Pass is perhaps best to be used as part of a loop ride from the Front Range rather than for real climbing.

Directions - In Granby on Route 40 head west a few miles to Route 125 on the right. The climb begins here by heading north on Route 125.

Rabbit Ears Pass West

Total elevation - 2,469 ft	**Length - 7.4 miles**
Average Grade - 6.3% (8%)	**Rating - 1.81 (cat 1)**

The west side of Rabbit Ears Pass is the big climb in the Steamboat Springs area. It is a solid ascent over steady grade on Route 40. The listed climb ends shy of the actual pass at the west summit. You will enjoy the descent as it is one of the fastest in the state. There is no real hill on the east side of Rabbit Ears.

Directions - In Steamboat Springs head east (true south) on Route 40 for several miles, soon passing Route 131 on the right. The climb begins shortly thereafter at the obvious grade change by continuing east on 40.

Gore Pass East

Total elevation - 1,685 ft	**Length - 6.9 miles**
Average Grade - 4.6% (7%)	**Rating - 0.91 (cat 2)**

The east side of Gore Pass is a pleasant climb on a narrow road with little traffic. A bit hot and dusty down low, the upper stretches are a nice ascent There is no real hill on the west side of Gore Pass.

Directions - Take Route 40 west (north) from Kremmling to Route 134 (left). Travel 134 west for just over 4 miles to begin the listed climb.

Southeast Colorado

Southeast Colorado is defined as the area west of Interstate 25, east of and including Routes 24 and 285 and south of Interstate 70.

Battle Mountain

Total elevation - 1,131 ft	**Length - 3.4 miles**
Average Grade - 6.3% (8%)	**Rating - 0.71 (cat 2)**

This is a pleasant and surprisingly stout climb that carries little traffic. Great views are present near the top which is unmarked but obvious.

Directions - From Interstate 70 west of Vail take Route 24 south through Minturn to the Eagle River where the listed climb begins.

Tennessee Pass North

Total elevation - 1,420 ft	**Length - 4.9 miles**
Average Grade - 5.5 (7%)	**Rating - 0.78 (cat 2)**

The north side of Tennessee Pass is a short and scenic climb. There is no real climb on the south side of the pass.

Directions - From Minturn on Route 24 head south over the Battle Mountain climb. Descend for a bit and then the road begins shallow climbing. The listed climb begins at the scenic lake and pullout on the left.

Fremont Pass North

Total elevation - 1,592 ft **Length - 10.7 miles**

Average Grade - 2.8% (7%) **Rating - 0.55 (cat 3)**

The north side of Fremont Pass is an overall shallow climb to high altitude from Copper Mountain on Interstate 70 west of Frisco. It has a shallow start and then you encounter a solid section of steady grade with great views. There is a bit of traffic on this hill but not enough to ruin the ride. Near the top the road rolls a bit over very shallow grade before you reach its signed summit (11,318 feet). Once you reach the steeper section this is a very fast descent as well.

Directions - From Copper Mountain on Interstate 70 head south on Route 91 for a very short distance to Copper Road (stop light) to being the listed climb.

Fremont Pass South

Total elevation - 1,320 ft **Length - 9.8 miles**

Average Grade - 2.6% (7%) **Rating - 0.41 (cat 3)**

The south side climb of Fremont Pass is a shallow but scenic climb up to high altitude. The pass is signed and there is a big mine at the top so watch for trucks.

Directions - In Leadville head north on Route 91 for several miles (descending a bit) to begin the climb where the road begins to head back up.

Hoosier Pass North

Total elevation - 1,894 ft | **Length - 9.7 miles**

Average Grade - 3.7% (6%) | **Rating - 0.86 (cat 2)**

The climb of the north side of Hoosier Pass is a very scenic route to high altitude (11,541 ft at summit). The first 6 miles are quite shallow but traffic is generally light. The last 3 miles are true alpine climbing with big mountain views in places and through switchbacks up to the signed pass.

Directions - In Breckinridge, CO the listed climb begins at Broken Lance Road on Route 9 as you leave town heading south.

Hoosier Pass South

Total elevation - 1,034 ft | **Length - 3.7 miles**

Average Grade - 5.3% (7%) | **Rating - 0.66 (cat 2)**

The south side of Hoosier Pass is a pleasant route to altitude along a somewhat straight and steady grade road. 100% of this one is above 10,000 feet so the altitude may affect some riders. The summit is a good place to stop for the views and it is a very fast and fun descent.

Directions - In Alma, CO head north on Route 9 for a short distance and cross the middle fork of the South Platte River. 1.3 miles later the listed climb begins at an obvious elevation change (dirt road on left).

Above 11,000 feet on Hoosier Pass

Scenery on the north side of Hoosier Pass

Loveland Pass North

Total elevation - 1,191 ft | **Length - 4.2 miles**
Average Grade - 5.4% (8%) | **Rating - 0.80 (cat 2)**

The north side of Loveland Pass is a spectacular ascent along a steady grade to high altitude. Fairly short, the route is never steep and carries a little traffic but not enough to ruin this hill. Near the top hair pin turns guide you upward and great views appear. At the top the pass is signed (11,992 ft) and this ascent is a challenging descent as well.

Directions - On Interstate 70 in Georgetown, CO head west to Route 6 and exit 216 (if you enter the Eisenhower Tunnel you have missed the exit). The climb begins at the bottom of the exit ramp by heading south on Route 6.

Loveland Pass South

Total elevation - 2,533 ft | **Length - 8.3 miles**
Average Grade - 5.8% (9%) | **Rating - 1.83 (cat 1)**

The south side of Loveland Pass is a solid climb up past a ski resort to very good views from the pass. Several switchbacks toward the top give it an alpine feel and it carries a steady grade up to the signed summit.

Directions - From Keystone, CO take Route 6 east for several miles to Montezuma Road (on the right) where the climb begins (grade change).

A rider on the climb to Loveland Pass

Views over the north side of Loveland Pass

Mount Evans

Total elevation - 6,590 ft	**Length - 27.8 miles**
Average Grade - 4.5% (10%)	**Rating - 3.88 (hors)**

The road on Mount Evans is the highest paved road in the northwestern hemisphere and the most difficult climb in Colorado. Never very steep, the altitude will work on you all the way up. The start is a bit congested and over shallow grade but signs of civilization soon end. After 13.2 fairly steady miles through a forest and just past Echo Lake turn right to pass through an entrance station for the push to the summit. The road steepens here and soon narrows as you soon head above the treeline. There are several small descents and spectacular views along an exposed road before you reach scenic Summit Lake Park at mile 21.5. The road climbs continuously from here (and over steeper grade) through switchbacks and alpine terrain with amazing views. At the top you will find an overlook and restrooms. You must hike the final bit to reach the very top of the mountain. Be careful on the descent as there are no guardrails in places and it is often very windy. Due to its altitude this road has a short window for use, usually opening by early June and closing sometime in September. It also carries a lot of traffic on good weather days so start early in the day. The toll booth is not manned after the road is closed in the Fall which often contains the best weather. This is a must do ride for serious hill climbers (top section closed in winter - Arapaho National Forest 303 567-3000).

Directions - From Interstate 70 in Idaho Springs, CO take exit 240 for Route 103. Head south on 103 and you immediately come to the Clear Creek Ranger Station on the right. The listed climb begins here.

High on Mount Evans

A switchback above 12,000 feet

Guanella Pass

Total elevation - 1,590 ft **Length - 5.8 miles**
Average Grade - 5.2% (10%) **Rating - 0.99 (cat 2)**

Guanella Pass is a nice climb close to Interstate 70. Soon after climbing begins you encounter some switchbacks which lift you up the ridge. The 2nd half has poor pavement in places and the road turns to dirt at the top of the listed climb which is short of the actual pass. The pavement and tight turns make for a tough descent in places.

Directions - In Georgetown, CO get to the intersection of Rose Street and Guanella Pass Road on the west edge of town and the climb begins shortly by heading up Guanella Pass Road.

Juniper Pass East

Total Elevation - 3,353 ft **Length - 16.0 miles**
Average Grade - 4.0% (6%) **Rating - 1.62 (cat 1)**

Another moderate grade and high altitude climb, the east side of Juniper Pass is very scenic in places. You may find more bikes on this road than autos on many days which is a nice change. The grade is steady and through thick woods almost all the way up and never steep.

Directions - From Bergen Parkway in the town of Bergen Park head west on Squaw Pass Road (Route 103) to begin the climb.

Juniper Pass West

Total elevation - 3,590 ft **Length - 15.9 miles**
Average Grade - 4.3% (7%) **Rating - 1.87 (cat 1)**

This climb shares its beginning with Mount Evans. At mile 13.2 (junction to Mount Evans) continue straight on Route 103. The hill crests 2.7 miles later at an unmarked pass. This high point on the road is not the actual Juniper Pass which is a ridge crest one mile behind you (and several hundred feet lower).

Directions - On I-70 in Idaho Springs, CO take exit 240 for Route 103. Head south and just after exiting you come to the Clear Creek Ranger Station on the right to begin the climb.

South Turkey Creek Road

Total elevation - 1,075 ft **Length - 7.9 miles**
Average Grade - 2.6% (8%) **Rating - 0.31 (cat 3)**

South Turkey Creek Road is another convenient climb near Route 285 close to Denver. Near the bottom you pass North Turkey Creek Road and Tiny Town. The 2nd half is twisty and more challenging and the road dead ends at Route 285. It is a fun descent as well. North Turkey Creek Road is also a shallow climb that begins 1.5 miles up South Turkey (7.1 miles at 2.7% average grade).

Directions - From Interstate 470 in Denver head west on Route 285 for several miles to South Turkey Creek Road on the left. The climb begins at this junction.

Deer Creek Canyon Road

Total elevation - 1,624 ft | **Length - 7.1 miles**
Average Grade - 4.3% (9%) | **Rating - 0.77 (cat 2)**

Deer Creek Canyon Road is a popular climb near the southwest side of Denver. A shallow start gradually leads to steeper grade along a narrow road within a twisty canyon. The listed climb ends at an obvious top (road on right) just before the road begins its descent to South Turkey Creek Road.

Directions - On Interstate 470 in southwest Denver exit to Wadsworth Road. Head south on Wadsworth for a short distance and turn right on Deer Creek Road. In two miles make a left to continue and to begin the listed climb.

South Deer Creek Canyon Road

Total elevation - 2,777 ft | **Length - 11.3 miles**
Average Grade - 4.7% (7%) | **Rating - 1.42 (cat 1/2)**

This climb shares its start with Deer Creek Canyon Road (previous climb). After 3-4 miles turn left on South Deer Creek Canyon Road. Never steep, you encounter a big switchback just over two miles from that junction. Near the end you feel like you are in the mountains as you ride through big pines across a mesa top. The listed climb ends just before the cyclist rest stop (porta potty) on the right.

Directions - See previous climb.

Kenosha Pass East

Total elevation - 2,212 ft **Length - 18.6 miles**
Average Grade - 2.3% (7%) **Rating - 0.59 (cat 2/3)**

The east side of Kenosha Pass is a long and shallow climb on Route 285 with traffic most of the time. Never steep, the grade is stair step up to the pass. There is no real climb on the west side. This one may be best as a descent.

Directions - In Bailey, CO on Route 285 the climb begins by heading west on 285.

Cottonwood Pass

Total elevation - 3,597 ft **Length - 13.5 miles**
Average Grade - 5.0% (10%) **Rating - 2.27 (cat 1)**

A long and solid climb, Cottonwood ends as one of the highest alpine passes (12,126 ft) in the United States. Down low the grade is quite shallow within a canyon. Aspens and elegant curves accompany you up the hill and it is surrounded by some of the biggest mountains in the state. Sections have solid grade and the road turns to dirt at the signed top (closed in winter - San Isabel National Forest - 719 539-3591). It is a challenging descent as well.

Directions - From Route 24 in Buena Vista, CO head west on Route 306 for ~5 miles (very shallow grade) to Route 343 on the left where the listed climb begins.

Trout Creek Pass West

Total elevation - 1,606 ft	**Length - 11.8 miles**
Average Grade - 2.6% (5%)	**Rating - 0.48 (cat 3)**

The west side of Trout Creek Pass is a shallow climb toward Antero Junction. There are good views of the big mountains to the west over its moderate grade but the route also includes fairly heavy traffic at times. There is no real climb on the east side of Trout Creek Pass.

Directions - From Buena Vista on Route 24head south for a short distance to Route 24/285. Head east on this road for a short distance to the Arkansas River where the listed climb begins.

Wilkerson Pass East

Total elevation - 1,625 ft	**Length - 9.8 miles**
Average Grade - 3.1% (7%)	**Rating - 0.59 (cat 2/3)**

The east side of Wilkerson Pass is a shallow climb up to a rest area at the summit (9,507 ft). Never steep the road carries some traffic most days. At the signed top there is rest area with parking. The west side of Wilkerson Pass is a short and unspectacular climb (~3.1 miles at 2.7%).

Directions - From Florissant head west on Route 24 for just over 5 miles to CO Route 77 on the right where the climb begins by continuing west on 24.

Near the top of Cottonwood Pass

Wilkerson Pass

Ute Pass East

Total elevation - 2,937 ft	**Length - 21.1 miles**
Average Grade - 2.6% (6%)	**Rating - 0.89 (cat 2)**

The east side of Ute Pass is a long and shallow climb from Colorado Springs. Four lane on Route 24 all the way, the steeper sections are on the lower end. As you can imagine there is traffic on the route. Never steep, the road does have room to ride over most of its length. It ends in the tiny town of Divide just beyond a stop light. It is actually a fun and fairly fast descent, particularly over its lower end.

Directions - From I-25 in Colorado Springs, CO head west on Route 24. After several miles you will come to the town of Manitou and the intersection with Manitou Road. The climb begins here by continuing west on 4-lane Route 24.

Ute Pass West

Total elevation - 1,011 ft	**Length - 8.5 miles**
Average Grade - 2.3% (5%)	**Rating - 0.26 (cat 3)**

The west side of Ute Pass is a shallow climb but at least it is a mountain road for much of its length. Two lanes and narrow, there is a bit of a shoulder to ride on but you will feel the traffic perhaps more on this side of the pass.

Directions - The climb begins at the west side of the small town of Florissant on Route 24 by heading east.

Pikes Peak

Total elevation - 3,872 ft	**Length - 15.7 miles**
Average Grade - 4.7% (10%)	**Rating - 2.11 (cat 1)**

Unfortunately this climb is closed to bikes (except for the hopefully annual race begun in 2010). After 5.3 miles on Route 24 turn left on Pikes Peak Highway. Soon after, keep left at a fork in the road. The grade increases and you soon pass the tollbooth. A steep mile follows and then the grade levels off. Passing a lake on the left, great views of the mountain appear. After another few miles the road turns to gravel.

Directions - In Colorado Springs head west on Route 24 to the town of Manitou and the intersection with Manitou Road. The climb begins here by continuing west on 4-lane Route 24.

Cheyenne Mountain Road

Total elevation - 1,228 ft	**Length - 3.3 miles**
Average Grade - 7.0% (12%)	**Rating - 1.23 (cat 1/2)**

Cheyenne Mountain is a great climb in Colorado Springs used by top cyclists at times. Narrow and twisty, it carries a solid grade getting steeper as you go generally. You pass scenic Helen Hunt Falls near the top. Above that point is steep climbing and the ascent ends where the pavement turns to dirt.

Directions - In Colorado Springs from Cheyenne Blvd and Cresta, head west on Cheyenne to the 4 way stop. The climb begins by bearing right toward Helen Hunt Falls.

Gold Camp

Total elevation - 841 ft	**Length - 4.4 miles**
Average Grade - 3.6% (9%)	**Rating - 0.33 (cat 3)**

The climb of Gold Camp in Colorado Springs, while not difficult, is a nice way to get a climb in right in town and has some good views up top. At just over a mile into the ascent turn left on Gold Camp Road for a flat section which blunts the average grade. Climbing soon resumes with views down on Colorado Springs and the listed climb ends where the pavement ends. A dirt road connects Gold Camp with the top of the previous climb (Cheyenne Mountain).

Directions - In Colorado Springs get to the intersection of 21st Street and Lower Gold Camp Road to begin the climb,

Poncha Pass North

Total elevation - 1,558 ft	**Length - 6.9 miles**
Average Grade - 4.3% (7%)	**Rating - 0.77 (cat 2)**

The north side of Poncha Pass is a fairly solid ascent along Route 285. A steady grade makes for a nice ride although there is a bit of traffic on this route. The road is within a canyon for much of its length. The grade and wide road makes for a nice descent as well. The south side is a less organized climb.

Directions - In Poncha Springs head south on Route 285 for a short distance to a creek crossing to begin the listed climb.

96 East

Total elevation - 2,947 ft | **Length - 13.8 miles**
Average Grade - 4.0% (7%) | **Rating - 1.37 (cat 1/2)**

The east side of Route 96 takes riders toward Hardscrabble Pass over a little travelled route and ends just shy of that pass. After just over 4 miles of variable grade climbing you enter a canyon and things get more scenic between rock walls in places. At its junction with Route 165 (left) remain west on 96. The grade continues to be moderate and the listed climb ends in another 4.1 miles at an unmarked summit.

Directions - In tiny Wetmore, CO the climb begins at the intersection of Routes 67 and 96 by heading west on 96.

Hardscrabble Pass West

Total elevation - 1,090 ft | **Length - 9.9 miles**
Average Grade - 2.1% (6%) | **Rating - 0.26 (cat 3)**

A very shallow climb, the west side of Hardscrabble Pass from Westcliffe is scenic with great views of the Sangre de Cristo Mountains in places. Little traffic and a mostly steady grade results in a pleasant ride. The grade over its 2nd half is a bit steeper and the listed climb ends at unmarked Hardscrabble Pass. Best part of this climb may be its descent which is pretty fast with good views.

Directions - In Westcliffe, CO head east on Route 96 to begin the listed climb.

96/165

Total elevation - 3,286 ft	Length - 14.1 miles
Average Grade - 4.4% (8%)	Rating - 1.68 (cat 1)

96/165 shares its beginning with 96 East. At the scenic junction of Routes 96 and 165 continue south on 165. This section soon enters the trees and has an isolated feel and is over moderate grade. The listed climb ends at an unmarked top 4.4 miles from the junction of 96 and 165. The road descends from there and then rolls up and down; pleasant riding but continuous climbing has ended.

Directions - In Wetmore, CO the climb begins at the intersection of Routes 67 and 96 by heading west on Route 96 to begin the climb.

165 South

Total elevation - 2,633 ft	Length - 13.6 miles
Average Grade - 3.7% (8%)	Rating - 1.12 (cat 2)

The climb of the south side of Route 165 is long and scenic. The grade is never steep and the route sees little traffic. About 10 miles in you pass a small lake and then the tiny community of San Isabel soon appears. The climb ends (unmarked) at Bishop Castle.

Directions - In Colorado City on Interstate 25 head west on Route 165 for several miles to the tiny town of Rye. The climb begins here by continuing west on 165.

Heading south on Route 165

The scenic west side of Hardscrabble Pass

North La Veta Pass East

Total elevation - 1,926 ft	**Length - 8.2 miles**
Average Grade - 4.4% (7%)	**Rating - 0.99 (cat 2)**

The east side of North La Veta Pass is a moderate climb along Route 160 with a bit of high speed traffic although there is plenty of room to ride. The route stair steps up the mountain to the unmarked but obvious summit. As the road is straight for most of its length the highlight of this one may be the descent and it is a fast one. Just keep an eye out for any 18 wheelers as you head down.

Directions - From Route 12 in La Veta, CO head west on Ryus Road (the road changes names along the way but no turns are involved) to Route 160. Head west on Route 160 for 1.6 miles to begin the listed climb.

North La Veta Pass West

Total elevation - 1,135 ft	**Length - 8.4 miles**
Average Grade - 2.6% (5%)	**Rating - 0.37 (cat 3)**

The west side of North La Veta Pass is a shallow ascent to altitude with some traffic primarily using the route to get from Alamosa over to Interstate 25. The road is wide however so vehicles are not a big bother.

Directions - In Fort Garland head east on Route 160 for 11.7 miles to begin the climb where the grade pops up.

Cucharas Pass North

Total elevation - 2,411 ft **Length - 16.3 miles**

Average Grade - 2.8% (7%) **Rating - 0.80 (cat 2)**

This is a shallow but stunning climb in the shadow of giant West Spanish Peak that dominates the skyline on the lower part of the ascent. Down low the road flows through a rock walled canyon over a shallow and variable grade. At mile 9.8 pass through tiny Cucharas within increasingly thick trees. You soon enter the national forest and the final section is classic alpine climbing.

Directions - In Walsenburg, CO on I-25 head west on Route 160 for ~11 miles to Route 12 (left). Travel Route 12 for ~5 miles to tiny La Veta. From the junction with Ryus in La Veta continue south on Route 12 for 1.2 miles to begin the climb where the road makes a 90 degree turn to the left.

Cucharas Pass South

Total elevation - 2,135 ft **Length - 15.2 miles**

Average Grade - 2.7 (8%) **Rating - 0.68 (cat 2)**

The south side of Cucharas Pass begins along a straight and stout road. The route then levels off a bit and you pass multiple lakes through thick woods. Several descents are encountered and the climb has an isolated feel. Near the top the trees thin and the top is unmarked but obvious.

Directions - In Trinidad, CO head west on Route 12 for ~32 miles to tiny Stonewall to begin the climb.

Western Colorado

Western Colorado is defined as the area west of Routes 24 and 285 to the Utah border. It includes many of the big mountains in the state along with scenic Route 550.

Belly Ache

Total elevation - 2,066 ft	**Length - 5.2 miles**
Average Grade - 7.5% (10%)	**Rating - 1.79 (cat 1)**

You may get one on this climb just west of Vail. Solid grade from the start, you pass a golf course down low. The grade then increases and you enter an area of homes. Views appear near the top and the climb ends where the pavement ends.

Directions - In Wolcott, CO on Interstate 70 take exit 157. Turn south and the climb begins at the cattle guard by heading south.

Squaw Creek Road

Total elevation - 1,094 ft	**Length - 4.1 miles**
Average Grade - 5.1% (10%)	**Rating - 0.62 (cat 2)**

Squaw Creek Road is a nice climb just south of I-70 near Edwards. A shallow start leads to steeper grade after a switchback. The listed climb ends at a private community.

Directions - From Route 6 in Edwards, CO head west for a few miles to Squaw Creek Road (left) where the climb begins.

Steep grade near the top of Bellyache

The view from Squaw Creek Road near Vail

Douglas Pass North

Total elevation - 1,173 ft **Length - 3.1 miles**

Average Grade - 7.2% (9%) **Rating - 0.95 (cat 2)**

The north side of Douglas Pass is an isolated climb north of Grand Junction in far western CO. An unmarked start leads to fairly steep switchback climbing up to the pass. Make sure you carry what you might need on this one.

Directions - In Rangely, CO on Route 64 head east on 64 for a short distance to Route 139. Head south on 139 for ~35 rolling miles to begin the listed climb.

Douglas Pass South

Total elevation - 1,467 ft **Length - 4.2 miles**

Average Grade - 6.6% (8%) **Rating - 1.09 (cat 2)**

The south side of Douglas Pass is a scenic climb in isolated terrain north of Grand Junction. The road quickly begins to switchback up the mountain. Its upper end is along a ridge with big rock walls and some exposure and ends at an obvious top. The road surprisingly carries some traffic at times (at least the day the author was on this hill). Due to its twisty nature it is a challenging descent as well.

Directions - In Loma, CO on Interstate 70 just west of Grand Junction, head north on Route 139 for just over 30 rolling miles to begin the listed climb (just beyond mile marker 30).

Near the top of Douglas Pass

Big rock walls heading up Douglas Pass

Colorado National Monument East

Total elevation - 1,900 ft	**Length - 8.4 miles**
Average Grade - 4.3% (8%)	**Rating - 0.88 (cat 2)**

Made famous in the movie American Flyers, this climb up the east side of the Monument is very scenic, passing through a short tunnel. There is a gate near the bottom which if manned may charge you for the climb. At mile 7.1 turn left toward Glade Park Store to continue to climb. The hill ends 1.3 miles later at an unmarked crest.

Directions - In Grand Junction, CO head to the corner of Monument Drive and Route 340 to begin the climb.

Colorado National Monument West

Total elevation - 1,352 ft	**Length - 5.8 miles**
Average Grade - 4.4% (8%)	**Rating - 0.63 (cat 2)**

Similar in grade and scenery to the east side, the west side of Colorado National Monument is a very pleasant climb up soaring sandstone walls through twisty turns. The listed climb ends at the Visitors Center with great views of the surrounding countryside. You can continue riding across the top of the mesa for several miles to descend the east side.

Directions - In Fruita, CO head south on Route 340 from Interstate 70 for several miles to Rim Rock Drive on the right where the listed climb begins.

141 East

Total elevation - 1,331 ft	**Length - 6.5 miles**
Average Grade - 3.9% (6%)	**Rating - 0.54 (cat 2/3)**

The east side of Route 141 is a shallow but scenic climb near Grand Junction with views of desert sandstone. Never steep, the route is narrow but with little traffic most days. The listed climb ends as the grade eases at a pullout on the right. The road continues to ascend intermittently but over very shallow grade.

Directions - In Grand Junction head south on Route 50 for several miles to Route 141 on the right. Travel 141 for 1.3 miles to begin the listed climb.

Near the top of 141 East

Lands End

Total elevation - 1,6248 ft | **Length - 9.0 miles**
Average Grade - 3.4% (7%) | **Rating - 0.60 (cat 2)**

Lands End is a nice climb between Grand Junction and Delta from Route 50. The bottom section is very shallow and at mile 2.9 bear left on Lands End Road. The grade gradually gets steeper over this section. Near the top a switchback or two gets you to the very top where the pavement turns to dirt. Continuing would take a mountain bike and solid legs. Lands End is a pretty fast descent as well.

Directions - In Grand Junction head south on Route 50 several miles beyond Route 41 to Kannah Creek Road on the left where the listed climb begins.

Bonham Reservoir

Total elevation - 2,193 ft | **Length - 7.3 miles**
Average Grade - 5.7% (9%) | **Rating - 1.40 (cat 1/2)**

The climb towards Bonham Reservoir is an isolated and challenging hill. After 1.9 miles turn left for a flat section which reduces its average grade. The final segment is straight and over steeper grade overall. The climb ends as the road enters Grand Mesa National Forest as the pavement ends. The upper section of this route is a very fast descent.

Directions - In tiny Colbran east of Mesa on Route 330 head south on 59 □ Road for 0.1 miles to 58 □ Road on the right. The climb begins there by taking 58 □ Road up the hill.

End of pavement on Lands End

Looking down the fast descent of Bonham Reservoir

Grand Mesa North

Total elevation - 5,622 ft	**Length - 21.4 miles**
Average Grade - 5.0% (7%)	**Rating - 3.39 (hors/cat 1)**

The north side of Grand Mesa in the western part of the state is a long and scenic ascent and may be the second most difficult climb in Colorado. It also carries the 2nd greatest elevation gain in the state. It is close to Interstate 70 so pretty convenient and worth a visit if you are in the area. Typically there is little traffic on this hill and you can enjoy the ride and scenery. There is a bit of steeper climbing at the beginning of the ascent and that ends quickly as you head through the small town of Mesa along Route 65 on a straight stretch of road. The grade eases somewhat after leaving town and the mesa looms in front of you. This section is very fast on the descent. Eventually you start to switchback up to the high country, passing big groves of aspens along the way, with views when the trees part. The grade remains fairly steady through this section; never steep but solid ascending at altitude. Near the top the switchbacks end and the grade eases as you head inland through thick trees near the crest of the mesa. The climb ends on top of Grand Mesa at the border of Mesa and Delta counties. In addition to being a big climb this is also a fast (down low) and challenging descent so be prepared before you tackle this one.

Directions - From Grand Junction, CO head east on Interstate 70 for a short distance to Route 65 (exit 49). Head south on 65 for approximately ten miles (nice ride, slight climb) to its junction with Route 330 (on the left) to begin the climb by continuing on 65 up the hill.

On the upper slopes of Grand Mesa

Steep grade ahead

Grand Mesa South

Total elevation - 4,752 ft | **Length - 20.7 miles**

Average Grade - 4.4% (6%) | **Rating - 2.50 (cat 1)**

This side of Grand Mesa is a very long and scenic climb. An unspectacular lower end gives way to ridge views and lakes once into the National Forest. You pass Grand Mesa Lodge near the top and the climb ends at the Mesa County line. Due to its length it can be a tough descent as well.

Directions - From Delta, CO head east on Route 92 to Route 65. Turn left on 65, cross the Gunnison River bridge and travel ~9 miles to the small town of Cedaredge where the climb begins at the intersection with Main Street.

McClure Pass North

Total elevation - 1,268 ft | **Length - 4.2 miles**

Average Grade - 5.7% (8%) | **Rating - 0.83 (cat 2)**

The north side of McClure Pass west of Aspen is a short but challenging ascent along Route 133. Its main attraction may be the scenery as you cruise along the Crystal River to get to its start. The initial climb is through some curves but soon the road becomes straight up to the pass. It is a fairly fast descent as well.

Directions - In Carbondale west of Aspen on Route 133 head south on Route 133 for ~22 miles to the dirt road to Marble on the left where the listed climb begins.

McClure Pass South

Total elevation - 1,914 ft | **Length - 7.7 miles**

Average Grade - 4.7% (7%) | **Rating - 1.02 (cat 2)**

The south side of McClure Pass is a bit longer and more shallow than its north side and over a straight road. The listed stats are estimates.

Directions - In Paonia, CO on Route 133 head north on 133 for ~29 miles to the large pullout where the listed climb begins.

Independence Pass East

Total elevation - 2,870 ft | **Length - 17.4 miles**

Average Grade - 3.1% (6%) | **Rating - 1.12 (cat 2)**

The east side of Independence Pass is a very spectacular alpine climb along Route 82 beginning in Twin Lakes. Shallow to start, the road meanders through the trees over its lower half with views at times and typically not much traffic. Closer to the top several big switchbacks provide increased grade and great views. Never particularly steep however, the route tops out above the tree line to finish at the signed pass. Independence Pass is the fourth highest paved road in Colorado. This is classis alpine ascending and a must do climb for cycling peak baggers.

Directions - In Twin Lakes, CO on Route 82 the climb begins at the west edge of town by continuing west on 82.

Independence Pass West

Total elevation - 3,991 ft	Length - 15.9 miles
Average Grade - 4.7% (7%)	Rating - 2.37 (cat 1)

The west side of Independence Pass is one of the most spectacular climbs in the United States. The first several miles are along a two lane road through thick trees. The grade is never steep on this hill but the altitude can make you work. Higher up the road narrows and hugs a cliff with great views. Returning to a wider road, a very scenic alpine section takes you up to the exposed pass at 12,095 feet (closed in winter - San Isabel National Forest - 719 539-3591).

Directions - From Aspen, CO head east on Route 82. After ~3.5 miles you will see a sign and parking area for the White River National Forest on the right. The listed climb begins here.

347

Total elevation - 1,987 ft	Length - 6.4 miles
Average Grade - 5.9% (7%)	Rating - 1.33 (cat 1/2)

This is an excellent climb leading into Black Canyon of the Gunnison National Park. The road contains a little bit of traffic but along a steady grade with good views. If you plan to do East Portal (next climb) this would be a good warm-up and it is a fun descent.

Directions - In Montrose, CO head east on Route 50 for ~ 8 miles to Route 347 on the left where the climb begins.

Great views on Independence Pass

A big switchback on Independence Pass

East Portal

Total elevation - 1,938 ft	**Length - 3.0 miles**
Average Grade - 12.2% (16%)	**Rating - 2.75 (hors/cat 1)**

East Portal is a very steep and dramatic climb up from the Gunnison River within Black Canyon of the Gunnison National Park. It is likely the steepest climb of any reasonable length in Colorado and one of the steepest in the United States. Enjoy the river (ride along it to the dam before you head out) and the pastoral setting at its start as you will be focusing on your pain level much of the way up. From the river head uphill on the narrow road. The first two miles are well beyond double digit grade and eventually involve several big switchbacks. A tight switchback contains the maximum grade on this ascent but the grade only eases slightly after the turn. There are nice views throughout and the slope finally begins to ease as you exit the steep canyon. The listed climb ends after 3.0 miles at an unmarked summit (small gate). The road continues to climb intermittently for another 1.5 miles but along very shallow grade. Due to its steep grade and tight nature East Portal is a difficult descent so watch the road heading down so you can enjoy the climb back out. There is pleasant riding within the park as well and you can use the climb into the national park (previous climb) from Route 50 as a warm-up.

Directions - From Montrose, CO head east on Route 50 for ~8 miles to Route 347 on the left. Take 347 up into the national park. At the entrance station turn right to East Portal. Head down the steep road all the way to the river. Where the road splits (left to ranger residences/right along the river) turn around to begin the climb by heading out of the canyon.

Steep East Portal

Big mountain views

Monarch Pass East

Total elevation - 3,177 ft	**Length - 11.5 miles**
Average Grade - 5.2% (8%)	**Rating - 2.03 (cat 1)**

The east side of Monarch Pass is a steady grade hill to high altitude. The road carries some traffic but there is room on the shoulder. Never steep you ride over fairly steady grade over the entire route and there is a store on top. This is a very fast descent as well. While the road can carry some traffic at times it is still one of the best alpine climbs in the state.

Directions - From Poncha Springs on Route 50 head west on 50 to Maysville. From here travel west for a short distance to Route 220 on the left to begin the listed climb.

Monarch Pass West

Total elevation - 2,769 ft	**Length - 8.9 miles**
Average Grade - 6.0% (7%)	**Rating - 2.04 (cat 1)**

Shorter and steeper than the approach from the east, this is a great alpine climb. The road winds up the left side of the canyon over a steady grade for the most part and the route can carry some traffic at times. There is a store on top to fuel up. This is also one of the great descents in Colorado.

Directions - From Gunnison, CO head east on Route 50 to the small town of Sargents. In Sargents continue east for 1.1 miles to a creek crossing (just before leaving Gunnison County) where the climb begins.

Views from the east side of Monarch Pass

Grade warning on Monarch West

North Pass East

Total elevation - 1,425 ft **Length - 5.7 miles**
Average Grade - 4.7% (7%) **Rating - 0.80 (cat 2)**

The east side of North Pass is a fairly short and isolated climb to altitude just south of Monarch Pass. Not as scenic as many Colorado climbs, this is nonetheless a good workout with an isolated feel. Near the top the grade steepens a bit and the top is unmarked but obvious. You will enjoy the good views of the San Luis Valley as you descend.

Directions - In Saguache, CO head west on Route 114 for just over 20 miles to begin the listed climb.

North Pass West

Total elevation - 1,171 ft **Length - 10.8 miles**
Average Grade - 2.1% (8%) **Rating - 0.27 (cat 3)**

The west side of North Pass is a fairly shallow climb south of Route 50 in central Colorado over narrow in places Route 114. A bit difficult to get to, once there the ride is pleasant as there is very little traffic to contend with. The author never made it to this ascent and thus these stats are estimates.

Directions - From the junction of Routes 50 and 114 just west of tiny Parlin, CO head south on 114 for ~20 miles to begin the listed climb right after a descent.

Dallas Divide East

Total elevation - 1,968 ft **Length - 10.3 miles**
Average Grade - 3.2% (7%) **Rating - 0.82 (cat 2)**

The east side climb of Dallas Divide starts in the town of Ridgway before heading up the ridge towards the west after a few small descents. A shallow climb for the most part, there is a bit of steeper grade closer to the top. The grade then eases near the summit but views abound on this one as there are few trees and the top is unmarked but obvious.

Directions - From the junction of Routes 550 and 62 in Ridgway head west on Route 62 for 0.4 miles to Railroad Road on the right to begin the ascent.

Dallas Divide West

Total elevation - 1,659 ft **Length - 12.3 miles**
Average Grade - 2.6% (6%) **Rating - 0.61 (cat 2)**

The west side of Dallas Divide is a long and shallow climb. Very shallow to start, the grade never really gets going on this one but it is a pleasant ascent. Down low the road is within a drainage but you break out of the canyon toward the top and views and aspens appear.

Directions - In Placerville, CO at the very compact and scenic junction of Routes 62 and 145, head east on Route 62 to begin the ascent.

Lizard Head Pass North

Total elevation - 1,552 ft | **Length - 11.7 miles**

Average Grade - 2.5% (6%) | **Rating - 0.46 (cat 3)**

While not a difficult ascent, the north side of Lizard Head Pass is one of the most spectacular routes in the world. After its start within some trees you soon come to a meadow and stunning views of peaked mountains. A descent follows back into the trees. Views soon reappear however. Never steep, the several descents knock down its average grade. The climb ends at the signed pass at over 10,000 feet.

Directions - In Telluride head west on Route 145 Spur for several miles to Route 145. Head south on 145 for 0.3 miles where the climb begins.

Lizard Head Pass South

Total elevation - 1,423 ft | **Length - 11.6 miles**

Average Grade - 2.3% (7%) | **Rating - 0.39 (cat 3)**

The south side of Lizard Head is a shallow climb with great scenery. The ride is over a narrow road much of the time but there is little traffic to worry about. The climb ends over very shallow grade at the pass with great views of the surrounding mountains.

Directions - The climb begins at the northern city limits of tiny Rico, CO on Route 145 by heading north on 145.

Big mountains toward Lizard Head

A descent on Lizard Head Pass

Mesa Verde National Park

Total elevation - 972 ft	**Length - 3.5 miles**
Average Grade - 5.3% (7%)	**Rating - 0.57 (cat 2/3)**

The climb into Mesa Verde National Park is a nice ascent with views of the surrounding mesas. It is over a twisty route with a few switchbacks and exposure in places. Never steep, near the top the grade eases and the climb ends at an unmarked top (road descends and then enters a tunnel). Due to the switchbacks and good pavement (as of 2010) Mesa Verde is a fun descent as well.

Directions - In Cortez, CO head east on Route 160 to the entrance for Mesa Verde National Park on the right. The listed climb begins at the end of the exit by heading south (right) toward the park.

160 East

Total elevation - 1,709 ft	**Length - 7.6 miles**
Average Grade - 4.3% (6%)	**Rating - 0.82 (cat 2)**

160 East is a climb from Durango up busy Route 160. Never steep, 160 carries a fair amount of traffic. The climb ends (unmarked) at a descent just before you reach the road to La Plata on the right.

Directions - In Durango, CO head west on Route 160 to the city limits to begin the listed climb.

Red Mountain Pass North

Total elevation - 3,200 ft	**Length - 12.5 miles**
Average Grade - 4.8% (8%)	**Rating - 1.89 (cat 1)**

This side of Red Mountain is a very spectacular climb up a twisty road to a high altitude pass (11,018 ft). This road is never steep but does carry a fair amount of traffic at times. A tale of three climbs perhaps, the lower end is particularly twisty with some exposure in places and stiffer grade. A straight section follows and the final segment contains multiple switchbacks. The grade eases near the top and this ascent may be along the most scenic, high mountain road in the U.S.

Directions - In downtown Ouray head south on Route 550 to the right hand turn that leads out of town and up the hill to begin the listed climb.

Red Mountain Pass South

Total elevation - 1,702 ft	**Length - 9.8 miles**
Average Grade - 3.3% (7%)	**Rating - 0.68 (cat 2)**

The south side of Red Mountain Pass, while not as scenic or challenging as its north side, is still a worthwhile climb. The route is fairly steady and can carry some traffic at times. The last 4 miles are more classic alpine climbing. The descent is quick back to Silverton.

Directions - The climb begins in tiny Silverton by heading north on Route 550.

Molas Pass North

Total elevation - 1,671 ft	**Length - 6.3 miles**
Average Grade - 5.0% (7%)	**Rating - 1.02 (cat 2)**

The north side of Molas Pass south of Silverton is one of the most scenic climbs in Colorado. Never steep, the first section goes right up the rocky ridge with views of the town and the Silverton to Durango railroad in the steep walled valley. After several miles you break out into a high valley that is surrounded with snow capped peaks. The grade is fairly steady throughout and the climb ends at the signed summit. The descent is a nice one with exposure in places.

Directions - In Silverton on Route 550 the climb begins at the bridge over Meadows Creek by continuing south on 550.

Molas Pass South

Total elevation - 1,123 ft	**Length - 4.2 miles**
Average Grade - 5.1% (7%)	**Rating - 0.69 (cat 2)**

The south side of Molas is a nice climb in an alpine setting along majestic Route 550. A twisty route makes for a pleasant ride but the road does carry some traffic most days. The smooth road (as of 2010) makes for a fun descent as well.

Directions - In Silverton, CO head south on Route 550 for ~10.5 miles (going over Molas Pass North in the process) to begin the climb by turning around and heading north up to the pass.

The top of Molas Pass

Exposure on the north side of Red Mountain

Coalbank Pass North

Total elevation - 843 ft	Length - 2.8 miles
Average Grade - 5.7% (7%)	**Rating - 0.58 (cat 2/3)**

The north side of Coalbank Pass is a short but pleasant ascent to a high altitude pass. The grade is steady and you will likely encounter some traffic on Route 550. It is a quick descent as well.

Directions - In Silverton, CO head south on Route 550 over Molas Pass. Descend the south side of Molas and the climb of the north side of Coalbank begins immediately.

Coalbank Pass South

Total elevation - 3,831 ft	Length - 20.1 miles
Average Grade - 3.6% (8%)	**Rating - 1.66 (cat 1)**

The south side of Coalbank is a long climb up to altitude. It is a stair step ascent but does carry some traffic. Good views help you to the top however. Once you pass Cascade Creek you encounter the most difficult climbing over the final stretch of the ascent. This final section is steep but steady and you will work to get through it. The pass is close however but within trees so views there are limited. There is a small rest stop on top. Its descent is intermittently fast.

Directions - In Hermosa, CO head north on Route 550 for ~3.5 miles to Route 250 on the right where the listed climb begins by continuing north on 550.

A warning on Coalbank Pass

Scenery to Coalbank Pass

Slumgullion Pass East

Total elevation - 1,084 ft	Length - 4.3 miles
Average Grade - 4.8% (5%)	Rating - 0.64 (cat 2)

The east side of Slumgullion Pass is an isolated, short and shallow ascent to altitude (11,530 ft). It is a scenic climb and over a steady grade. Thick trees accompany you up the hill but very little traffic makes for a pleasant ascent.

Directions - Ride over Slumgullion from the north side (next climb. After the descent the the east side turn around and climb back to the summit. Coming from the south is a very long ride from the tiny town of Creede on Route 149.

Slumgullion Pass West

Total elevation - 2,476 ft	Length - 7.7 miles
Average Grade - 6.1% (9%)	Rating - 1.86 (cat 1)

The west side of Slumgullion Pass is an isolated, high altitude climb (11,530 ft) with a grade that will make you work. Good views of the surrounding mountains when the trees thin can help get you to the top. There are several ramps of solid grade along the way but the grade eases near the top to finish at the signed summit.

Directions - From Lake City, CO head south on Route 149 to the bridge over the Lake Fork of the Gunnison River where the climb begins.

Wolf Creek Pass North

Total elevation - 2,271 ft	**Length - 9.4 miles**
Average Grade - 4.6% (6%)	**Rating - 1.26 (cat 1/2)**

The north side of Wolf Creek Pass is a pleasant ascent with some traffic. Shallow to start, one lane uphill soon leads to two along increasing grade. There is a snow shed near the top with a sharp left turn within it. The top is obvious and the descent is pretty quick.

Directions - In South Fork, CO on Route 160 head south on 160 for 9.5 shallow grade miles to begin the listed climb (pullout on the right).

Wolf Creek Pass South

Total elevation - 2,943 ft	**Length - 8.5 miles**
Average Grade - 6.6% (7%)	**Rating - 2.33 (cat 1)**

The more difficult side of Wolf Creek Pass, this climb is surprising challenging. There is a big switchback near the start and then the road straightens as it climbs the ridge. This route can carry some traffic at times but the road is wide so it does not ruin the ride. A steady grade and great views can help get you to the top. The descent is a burner but just watch out for the switchbacks down low.

Directions - In Pagosa Springs, CO head north on Route 160 for ~15 miles to West Fork Road on the left (just as the road heads up the hill) to begin the listed climb.

Cumbres Pass South

Total elevation - 2,1059 ft	**Length - 11.2 miles**
Average Grade - 3.6% (6%)	**Rating - 0.88 (cat 2)**

This climb begins in New Mexico but its summit is in Colorado. A shallow grade offers good mountain views and occasional crossings of the railroad tracks that head to the summit. The pass is signed and there is usually some train activity there. This is a pretty fast descent as well (watch the train crossings). The north side of Cumbres Pass is a very short climb.

Directions - In Chama, New Mexico head north through town on Route 17. The listed climb begins just beyond the railroad tracks as you leave town.

La Manga Pass North

Total elevation - 1,393 ft	**Length - 4.2 miles**
Average Grade - 6.3% (9%)	**Rating - 1.03 (cat 2)**

The north side of La Manga Pass is one of the most scenic in Colorado. Never really steep, the views will get to the top. At the listed climb end the grade eases dramatically. The road continues up to La Manga Pass but over shallow grade. The south side of La Manga is not much of a climb.

Directions - In Antonito, CO on Route 285 head west on Route 17 for ~25 miles to the Conejos River to begin the listed climb by continuing south up the hill.

The top of Cumbres Pass

Scenic views toward La Manga Pass

Organized Races/Rides with Significant Climbing

Bob Cook Memorial Mount Evans Hill Climb - The oldest hill climb race in the U.S. is usually held in late July (see climb description). For details go to http://bicyclerace.com.

Lookout Mountain Hill Climb - Many Colorado cyclists know their best time from 'pillar to post' up this hill. For details go to http://searcycling.org.

Mike Horgan Hill Climb - A tough climbing race that uses Boulder Canyon and Sugarloaf that includes dirt sections. For details go to http://boulderracing.com/horgan.asp.

Triple Bypass - A difficult ride from Evergreen to Avon over 3 big alpine passes including Loveland Pass. For details go to http://teamevergreen.org/triple.

Ride For the Pass - A charity race/ride of the incredibly scenic west side of Independence Pass near Aspen. For details go to http://independencepass.org/ridepass.htm.

Ironhorse Bicycle Classic - An annual event with different races that include big climbing around Durango. For details go to http://ironhorsebicycleclassic.com/events.

Copper Triangle - An annual ride that includes three high altitude climbs near Copper Mountain. For details go to http://coppertriangle.com/info.html.

A clear day in the Rockies

High mountain warning

50 Most Difficult Climbs (Author Rating; Major Tour Rating)

1.	Mount Evans	(3.88; hors)
2.	Grand Mesa North	(3.39; hors/cat 1)
3.	Trail Ridge East	(2.83; hors/cat 1)
4.	East Portal	(2.75; hors/cat 1)
5.	Grand Mesa South	(2.50; cat 1)
6.	Magnolia Road	(2.40; cat 1)
7.	Independence Pass West	(2.37; cat 1)
8.	Wolf Creek Pass South	(2.33; cat 1)
9.	Cottonwood Pass	(2.27; cat 1)
10.	Pikes Peak	(2.11; cat 1)
11.	Monarch Pass West	(2.04; cat 1)
12.	Monarch Pass East	(2.03; cat 1)
13.	Red Mountain Pass North	(1.89; cat 1)
14.	Juniper Pass West	(1.87; cat 1)
15.	Slumgullion Pass West	(1.85; cat 1)
16.	Loveland Pass South	(1.82; cat 1)
17.	Rabbit Ears Pass West	(1.81; cat 1)
18.	Belly Ache	(1.79; cat 1)
19.	Flagstaff Mountain	(1.77; cat 1)
20.	Lefthand Canyon/Ward Road	(1.77; cat 1)
21.	Sugarloaf Road	(1.70; cat 1)
22.	96/165	(1.68; cat 1)
23.	Coalbank Pass South	(1.66; cat 1)
24.	Rist Canyon East	(1.64; cat 1)
25.	Juniper Pass East	(1.62; cat 1)

Most Difficult Climbs Continued:

26. Super James (1.55; cat 1)
27. Lee Hill/Deer Trail Road (1.52; cat 1)
28. Golden Gate Canyon (1.47; cat 1/2)
29. South Deer Creek Canyon (1.46; cat 1/2)
30. Bonham Reservoir (1.40; cat 1/2)
31. 96 East (1.37; cat 1/2)
32. 347 (1.33; cat 1/2)
33. Berthoud Pass South (1.32; cat 1/2)
34. Trail Ridge West (1.30; cat 1/2)
35. Wolf Creek Pass North (1.26; cat 1/2)
36. 7 East (1.16; cat 2)
37. Boulder Canyon (1.13; cat 2)
38. Independence Pass East (1.12; cat 2)
39. 165 South (1.12; cat 2)
40. Berthoud Pass North (1.10; cat 2)
41. Douglas Pass South (1.09; cat 2)
42. Sunshine Canyon (1.05; cat 2)
43. Coal Creek Canyon East (1.04; cat 2)
44. La Manga Pass North (1.03; cat 2)
45. McClure Pass South (1.03; cat 2)
46. 119 (1.03; cat 2)
47. Molas Pass North (1.02; cat 2)
48. North La Veta Pass East (0.99; cat 2)
49. Guanella Pass (0.99; cat 2)
50. 36 East (0.95; cat 2)

Most Difficult Climbs by Distance

< 5 miles

1. East Portal
2. Magnolia Road
3. Flagstaff Mountain
4. Sugarloaf Road
5. Douglas Pass South

5-10 miles

1. Wolf Creek Pass South
2. Monarch Pass West
3. Slumgullion Pass West
4. Loveland Pass South
5. Rabbit Ears Pass West

10-15 miles

1. Cottonwood Pass
2. Monarch Pass East
3. Red Mountain Pass North
4. Lefthand Canyon/Ward Road
5. 96-165

Most Difficult Climbs by Distance (continued)

15-20 miles

1. Trail Ridge East
2. Independence Pass West
3. Pikes Peak
4. Juniper Pass West
5. Juniper Pass East

> 20 miles

1. Mount Evans
2. Grand Mesa North
3. Grand Mesa South
4. Coal Bank Pass South
5. Trail Ridge West

Additional Climbing Categories

Greatest Elevation Gain Climbs

1.	Mount Evans	- 6,590 ft
2.	Grand Mesa North	- 5,622 ft
3.	Grand Mesa South	- 4,752 ft
4.	Trail Ridge East	- 4,661 ft
5.	Independence Pass West	- 3,991 ft
6.	Cold Bank Pass South	- 3,831 ft
7.	Trail Ridge Pass West	- 3,814 ft
8.	Pikes Peak	- 3,796 ft
9.	Cottonwood Pass	- 3,597 ft
10.	Juniper Pass West	- 3,590 ft

Highest Elevation Attained Climbs

1.	Mount Evans	- 14,130 ft
2.	Trial Ridge	- 12,183 ft
3.	Cottonwood Pass	- 12,126 ft
4.	Independence Pass	- 12,095 ft
5.	Loveland Pass	- 11,992 ft
6.	Hoosier Pass	- 11,541 ft
7.	Slumgullion Pass	- 11,530 ft
8.	Fremont Pass	- 11,320 ft
9.	Monarch Pass	- 11,312 ft
10.	Berthoud Pass	- 11,307 ft

Additional Climbing Categories

Longest Climbs (> 3% average grade)

1. Mount Evans - 27.8 miles
2. Grand Mesa North - 21.4 miles
3. Grand Mesa South - 20.7 miles
4. Coal Bank Pass South - 20.1 miles
5. Trail Ridge East - 18.2 miles
6. Independence Pass East - 17.4 miles
7. Juniper Pass East - 16.0 miles
8. Independence Pass West - 15.9 miles
9. Juniper Pass West - 15.9 miles
10. Pikes Peak - 15.7 miles

Steepest Climbs (min 2.0 miles in length)

1. East Portal - 12.2%
2. Magnolia Road - 9.1%
3. Flagstaff Road - 8.1%
4. Sunshine Canyon - 7.8%
5. Sugarloaf Road - 7.7%
6. Belly Ache - 7.6%
7. Douglas Pass North - 7.2%
8. Cheyenne Mountain - 7.0%
9. Douglas Pass South - 6.6%
10. Wolf Creek Pass South - 6.6%

Additional Climbing Categories

Climbs with Greatest Length of 10%+ Grade

1.	East Portal	- 2.6 miles
2.	Magnolia Road	- 1.9 miles
3.	Flagstaff Mountain	- 1.7 miles
4.	Lee Hill/Deer Trail Road	- 1.1 miles
5.	Rist Canyon West	- 1.0 miles
6.	Lefthand Canyon/Ward Road	- 0.7 miles
7.	Sugarloaf Road	- 0.7 miles
8.	Sunshine Canyon	- 0.5 miles
9.	Rist Canyon East	- 0.5 miles
10.	Golden Gate Canyon	- 0.5 miles

Most Technical Descents

1. East Portal
2. Magnolia Road
3. Flagstaff Mountain
4. Mount Evans
5. Red Mountain Pass North
6. Belly Ache
7. Colorado National Monument East
8. Slumgullion Pass West
9. Sugarloaf Road
10. Sunshine Canyon

Additional Climbing Categories

Fastest Descents

1. Rabbit Ears Pass West
2. Wolf Creek Pass South
3. Hoosier Pass South
4. Rist Canyon West
5. Monarch Pass West
6. Fremont Pass North
7. Monarch Pass East
8. Cumbres Pass South
9. Bonham Reservoir
10. Lands End

Most Scenic/Spectacular Climbs

1. Red Mountain Pass North
2. Lizard Head Pass North
3. Independence Pass West
4. Trail Ridge Pass East
5. Mount Evans
6. Loveland Pass North
7. Colorado National Monument West
8. East Portal
9. Independence Pass East
10. La Manga Pass North

Additional Climbing Resources

Books

Ascent, The Mountains of the Tour de France by Richard Yates, Cycle Publishing.
Cycling Colorado's Mountain Passes by Kurt Magsamen, Fulcrum Publishing, Golden, CO.
Kings of the Mountains by Matt Rendell, Arum Press. London, England.
The Complete Guide to Climbing (By Bike) by John Summerson, Extreme Press.
The Complete Guide to Climbing (By Bike) in California by John Summeson, Extreme Press.
The Complete Guide to Climbing (By Bike) in the Southeast by John Summeson, Extreme Press.
Uphill Battle by Owen Mulholland, Velopress, Boulder, CO.

Magazines

Bicycling
Cycle Sport America
Pro Cycling
Road
Road Bike Action
Velonews

Selected websites

Bicyling.com
Bikeradar.com
Cyclingnews.com
Dailypeloton.com

Spectacular East Portal

Missingsaddle.com
Northeastcycling.com
Roadcycling.com
Spokepost.com
Steephill.tv
Truesport.com
Usacycling.org
Utahcycling.com
Velonews.com
Westernwheelers.org

Training

AthletiCamps.com
Bicyclecoach.com
Bikecamp.com
Carmichael Training Systems (trainright.com)
Cycle-Smart.com
Cyclist Training Bible by Joe Friel, Velopress, Boulder, CO.
Eddie B. Cycling World Fitness (Eddiebcyclingworld.com)
EliteFITcoach.com
Tecknowlogysource.com
Peakscoachinggroup.com
Trainingpeaks.com

Forums

Bicycle.com
BikeForums.net
Bikeradar.com
CyclingForums.com
Dailypeloton.com
Forums.roadbikereview.com

Tinmtn.org - (Mount Washington Hill Climb Forum)
Sports.yahoo.com
Velonews.com

Touring

Adventure Cycling Association (aventurecycling.org)
Breaking Away Bicycle Tours (breakingaway.com)
Carpenter/Phinney Bike Camp (bikecamp.com)
Cycle America (cycleamerica.com)
Cycle Tours of Italy (cycleitalia.com)
Timberline Adventures (timbertours.com)
Trek Travel Cycling Vacations (trektravel.com)
Velo Classic Tours (veloclassictours.com)

Events

303cycling.com
Active.com
Americancycling.org
Azcycling.com
Bicyclecolo.org
Bikereg.com
Bikeride.com
Boulderbikerace.com
Coloradobicyclerides.com
Cycleidaho.com
Montanacycling.org
Northeastcycling.com
Nmcycling.com
Utahcycling.com

Additional Climbs Data Keys

Traffic:

1 – Almost nonexistent traffic
2 – Some traffic, mostly local
3 – Moderate to heavy traffic

Descent:

1 – Fast and smooth
2 – Fast with a few obstacles
3 – Speed somewhat blunted by obstacles (turns, traffic, etc)
4 – Difficult due to road and/or traffic conditions
5 – Danger of bodily harm at almost any speed

Views from the top of Belly Ache

Colorado Climbs Additional Data

Northeast Colorado

Cameron Pass East

Total elevation:	2,239 ft	Length:	12.1mi
Top elevation:	10,276 ft	Average grade:	3.5%
Minimum grade:	0%	Maximum grade:	6%
Distance ≥ 5%:	2.5 miles	Distance ≥ 10%:	0.0 mi
Steepest mile:	5.1%	Steepest 3 miles:	4.9%
Traffic:	2	Descent:	3

Cameron Pass West

Total elevation:	1,265 ft	Length:	7.9 mi
Top elevation:	10,276 ft	Average grade:	3.0%
Minimum grade:	0%	Maximum grade:	5%
Distance ≥ 5%:	2.2 miles	Distance ≥ 10%:	0.0 mi
Steepest mile:	4.8%	Steepest 3 miles:	4.5%
Traffic:	2	Descent:	3

Rist Canyon East

Total elevation:	2,813 ft	Length:	10.5 mi
Top elevation:	8,007 ft	Average grade:	5.1%
Minimum grade:	0%	Maximum grade:	13%
Distance > 5%:	5.7 miles	Distance > 10%:	0.5 mi
Steepest mile:	8.1%	Steepest 3 miles:	6.6%
Traffic:	1	Descent:	3

Rist Canyon West

Total elevation:	677 ft	Length:	1.4 mi
Top elevation:	8,007 ft	Average grade:	9.2%
Minimum grade:	2%	Maximum grade:	12%
Distance ≥ 5%:	1.2 miles	Distance ≥ 10%:	1.0 mi
Steepest mile:	10.8%	Steepest 3 miles:	NA
Traffic:	1	Descent:	1

Trail Ridge East

Total elevation:	4,661 ft	Length:	18.2 mi
Top elevation:	12,183 ft	Average grade:	4.9%
Minimum grade:	0%	Maximum grade:	7%
Distance ≥ 5%:	8.2 miles	Distance ≥ 10%:	0.0 mi
Steepest mile:	6.4%	Steepest 3 miles:	5.8%
Traffic:	3	Descent:	3

The top of steep Rist Canyon

The top of Red Mountain Pass

Trail Ridge West

Total elevation:	3,814 ft	Length:	26.5 mi
Top elevation:	12,183 ft	Average grade:	2.7%
Minimum grade:	0%	Maximum grade:	6%
Distance ≥ 5%:	10.6 miles	Distance ≥ 10%:	0.0 mi
Steepest mile:	5.9%	Steepest 3 miles:	5.4%
Traffic:	2	Descent:	3

Big Thompson Canyon

Total elevation:	2,196 ft	Length:	17.4 mi
Top elevation:	7,522 ft	Average grade:	2.4%
Minimum grade:	0%	Maximum grade:	6%
Distance ≥ 5%:	3.6 miles	Distance ≥ 10%:	0.0 mi
Steepest mile:	4.8%	Steepest 3 miles:	4.1%
Traffic:	3	Descent:	3

36 East

Total elevation:	2,678 ft	Length:	16.0 mi
Top elevation:	8,052 ft	Average grade:	3.2%
Minimum grade:	0%	Maximum grade:	7%
Distance ≥ 5%:	6.5 miles	Distance ≥ 10%:	0.0 mi
Steepest mile:	5.6%	Steepest 3 miles:	5.2%
Traffic:	3	Descent:	3

7 East

Total elevation:	2,749 ft	Length:	13.8 mi
Top elevation:	8,219 ft	Average grade:	3.8%
Minimum grade:	0%	Maximum grade:	8%
Distance ≥ 5%:	4.6 miles	Distance ≥ 10%:	0.0 mi
Steepest mile:	6.7%	Steepest 3 miles:	5.4%
Traffic:	2	Descent:	2

Lefthand Canyon/Ward Road

Total elevation:	3,361 ft	Length:	14.4 mi
Top elevation:	9,266 ft	Average grade:	4.4%
Minimum grade:	1%	Maximum grade:	12%
Distance ≥ 5%:	7.6 miles	Distance ≥ 10%:	0.7 mi
Steepest mile:	9.1%	Steepest 3 miles:	6.8%
Traffic:	2	Descent:	3

Super James

Total elevation:	2,617 ft	Length:	9.5 mi
Top elevation:	8,522 ft	Average grade:	5.2%
Minimum grade:	2%	Maximum grade:	11%
Distance ≥ 5%:	5.5 miles	Distance ≥ 10%:	0.1 mi
Steepest mile:	7.6%	Steepest 3 miles:	7.2%
Traffic:	1	Descent:	3

Lee Hill/Deer Trail Road

Total elevation:	2,077 ft	Length:	6.0 mi
Top elevation:	7,725 ft	Average grade:	6.6%
Minimum grade:	0%	Maximum grade:	16%
Distance ≥ 5%:	5.2 miles	Distance ≥ 10%:	1.1 mi
Steepest mile:	10.6%	Steepest 3 miles:	7.3%
Traffic:	2	Descent:	4

Sunshine Canyon

Total elevation:	1,242 ft	Length:	3.0 mi
Top elevation:	6,753 ft	Average grade:	7.8%
Minimum grade:	0%	Maximum grade:	12%
Distance ≥ 5%:	2.6 miles	Distance ≥ 10%:	0.5 mi
Steepest mile:	8.5%	Steepest 3 miles:	7.8 mi
Traffic:	1	Descent:	4

Four Mile Canyon

Total elevation:	1,210 ft	Length:	5.6 mi
Top elevation:	6,945 ft	Average grade:	4.1%
Minimum grade:	0%	Maximum grade:	9%
Distance ≥ 5%:	2.4 miles	Distance ≥ 10%:	0.0 mi
Steepest mile:	6.1%	Steepest 3 miles:	4.8%
Traffic:	1	Descent:	3

A warning in Boulder Canyon

Views from near the top of Lands End

Boulder Canyon

Total elevation:	2,101 ft	Length:	13.3 mi
Top elevation:	3,771 ft	Average grade:	3.8%
Minimum grade:	1%	Maximum grade:	10%
Distance ≥ 5%:	2.9 miles	Distance ≥ 10%:	0.1 mi
Steepest mile:	7.9%	Steepest 3 miles:	6.5%
Traffic:	2	Descent:	3

Sugar Loaf Road

Total elevation:	1,960 ft	Length:	4.8 mi
Top elevation:	8,069 ft	Average grade:	7.7%
Minimum grade:	0%	Maximum grade:	12%
Distance ≥ 5%:	3.7 miles	Distance ≥ 10%:	0.7 mi
Steepest mile:	8.8%	Steepest 3 miles:	8.2%
Traffic:	1	Descent:	3

Magnolia Road

Total elevation:	2,170 ft	Length:	4.5 mi
Top elevation:	8,237 ft	Average grade:	9.1%
Minimum grade:	0%	Maximum grade:	17%
Distance ≥ 5%:	3.8 miles	Distance ≥ 10%:	1.9 mi
Steepest mile:	11.6%	Steepest 3 miles:	8.4%
Traffic:	1	Descent:	5

Lower Magnolia Road

Exposure on Red Mountain

Flagstaff Mountain

Total elevation:	1,968 ft	Length:	4.6 mi
Top elevation:	7,696 ft	Average grade:	8.1%
Minimum grade:	4%	Maximum grade:	14%
Distance ≥ 5%:	4.4 miles	Distance ≥ 10%:	1.7 mi
Steepest mile:	10.7%	Steepest 3 miles:	8.8%
Traffic:	2	Descent:	5

NCAR

Total elevation:	683 ft	Length:	2.5 mi
Top elevation:	6,110 ft	Average grade:	5.2%
Minimum grade:	1%	Maximum grade:	9%
Distance ≥ 5%:	1.2 miles	Distance ≥ 10%:	0.0 mi
Steepest mile:	7.3%	Steepest 3 miles:	NA
Traffic:	2	Descent:	2

Coal Creek Canyon East

Total elevation:	2,009 ft	Length:	8.4 mi
Top elevation:	8,668 ft	Average grade:	4.5%
Minimum grade:	0%	Maximum grade:	7%
Distance ≥ 5%:	2.7 miles	Distance ≥ 10%:	0.0 mi
Steepest mile:	6.6%	Steepest 3 miles:	6.2%
Traffic:	1	Descent:	3

Golden Gate Canyon Road

Total elevation:	2,739 ft	Length:	11.3 mi
Top elevation:	8,688 ft	Average grade:	4.6%
Minimum grade:	0%	Maximum grade:	11%
Distance ≥ 5%:	5.4 miles	Distance ≥ 10%:	0.5 mi
Steepest mile:	8.7%	Steepest 3 miles:	6.5%
Traffic:	1	Descent:	3

Lookout Mountain Road

Total elevation:	1,438 ft	Length:	5.1 mi
Top elevation:	7,318 ft	Average grade:	5.3%
Minimum grade:	1%	Maximum grade:	7%
Distance ≥ 5%:	2.4 miles	Distance ≥ 10%:	0.0 mi
Steepest mile:	5.7%	Steepest 3 miles:	5.4%
Traffic:	2	Descent:	3

119

Total elevation:	2,426 ft	Length:	12.6 mi
Top elevation:	9,353 ft	Average grade:	3.6%
Minimum grade:	0%	Maximum grade:	7%
Distance ≥ 5%:	2.9 miles	Distance ≥ 10%:	0.0 mi
Steepest mile:	5.6%	Steepest 3 miles:	4.5%
Traffic:	2	Descent:	3

Berthoud Pass North

Total elevation:	2,197 ft	Length:	10.2 mi
Top elevation:	11,307 ft	Average grade:	4.1%
Minimum grade:	1%	Maximum grade:	6%
Distance ≥ 5%:	2.7 miles	Distance ≥ 10%:	0.0 mi
Steepest mile:	5.0%	Steepest 3 miles:	4.7%
Traffic:	2	Descent:	3

Berthoud Pass South

Total elevation:	2,524 ft	Length:	11.2 mi
Top elevation:	11,307 ft	Average grade:	4.3%
Minimum grade:	2%	Maximum grade:	6%
Distance ≥ 5%:	3.8 miles	Distance ≥ 10%:	0.0 mi
Steepest mile:	5.4%	Steepest 3 miles:	5.2%
Traffic:	2	Descent:	3

Willow Creek Pass North

Total elevation:	1,063 ft	Length:	9.8 mi
Top elevation:	9,683 ft	Average grade:	2.1%
Minimum grade:	0%	Maximum grade:	5%
Distance ≥ 5%:	3.4 miles	Distance ≥ 10%:	0.0 mi
Steepest mile:	5.5%	Steepest 3 miles:	5.1%
Traffic:	1	Descent:	3

Top of Berthoud Pass

Looking north from Berthoud Pass

Willow Creek Pass South

Total elevation:	1,832 ft	Length:	21.7 mi
Top elevation:	9,683 ft	Average grade:	1.6%
Minimum grade:	0%	Maximum grade:	5%
Distance ≥ 5%:	2.2 miles	Distance ≥ 10%:	0.0 mi
Steepest mile:	5.1%	Steepest 3 miles:	4.6%
Traffic:	1	Descent:	3

Rabbit Ears Pass West

Total elevation:	2,469 ft	Length:	7.4 mi
Top elevation:	9,394 ft	Average grade:	6.3%
Minimum grade:	3%	Maximum grade:	8%
Distance ≥ 5%:	6.5 miles	Distance ≥ 10%:	0.0 mi
Steepest mile:	6.8%	Steepest 3 miles:	6.5%
Traffic:	3	Descent:	1

Gore Pass East

Total elevation:	1,685 ft	Length:	6.9 mi
Top elevation:	9,527 ft	Average grade:	4.6%
Minimum grade:	1%	Maximum grade:	7%
Distance ≥ 5%:	3.1 miles	Distance ≥ 10%:	0.0 mi
Steepest mile:	5.6%	Steepest 3 miles:	5.3%
Traffic:	1	Descent:	3

Southeast Colorado

Battle Mountain North

Total elevation:	1,140 ft	Length:	3.4 mi
Top elevation:	8,095 ft	Average grade:	6.4%
Minimum grade:	3%	Maximum grade:	8%
Distane ≥ 5%:	2.9 miles	Distance ≥ 10%:	0.0 mi
Steepest mile:	6.7%	Steepest 3 miles:	6.5 mi
Traffic:	2	Descent:	2

Tennessee Pass North

Total elevation:	1,128 ft	Length:	4.9 mi
Top elevation:	10,424 ft	Average grade:	4.4%
Minimum grade:	2%	Maximum grade:	7%
Distance ≥ 5%:	3.2 miles	Distance ≥ 10%:	0.0 mi
Steepest mile:	5.7%	Steepest 3 miles:	5.4%
Traffic:	2	Descent:	3

Fremont Pass North

Total elevation:	1,592 ft	Length:	10.7 mi
Top elevation:	11,320 ft	Average grade:	2.8%
Minimum grade:	0%	Maximum grade:	7%
Distance ≥ 5%:	4.3 miles	Distance ≥ 10%:	0.0 mi
Steepest mile:	7.0%	Steepest 3 miles:	6.3%
Traffic:	2	Descent:	2

Fremont Pass South

Total elevation:	1,321 ft	Length:	9.8 mi
Top elevation:	11,320 ft	Average grade:	2.6%
Minimum grade:	1%	Maximum grade:	7%
Distance ≥ 5%:	2.7 miles	Distance ≥ 10%:	0.0 mi
Steepest mile:	4.9%	Steepest 3 miles:	4.7%
Traffic:	2	Descent:	3

Hoosier Pass North

Total elevation:	1,894 ft	Length:	9.7 mi
Top elevation:	11,541 ft	Average grade:	3.7%
Minimum grade:	0%	Maximum grade:	7%
Distance ≥ 5%:	4.7 miles	Distance ≥ 10%:	0.0 mi
Steepest mile:	6.3%	Steepest 3 miles:	6.0%
Traffic:	2	Descent:	3

Views from the top

Stats on Fremont Pass

Hoosier Pass South

Total elevation:	1,034 ft	Length:	3.7 mi
Top elevation:	11,541 ft	Average grade:	5.3%
Minimum grade:	3%	Maximum grade:	7%
Distance ≥ 5%:	3.2 miles	Distance ≥ 10%:	0.0 mi
Steepest mile:	5.8%	Steepest 3 miles:	5.5%
Traffic:	2	Descent:	1

Loveland Pass North

Total elevation:	1,191 ft	Length:	4.3 mi
Top elevation:	11,992 ft	Average grade:	5.4%
Minimum grade:	3%	Maximum grade:	8%
Distance ≥ 5%:	3.6 miles	Distance ≥ 10%:	0.0 mi
Steepest mile:	6.2%	Steepest 3 miles:	6.1%
Traffic:	2	Descent:	3

Loveland Pass South

Total elevation:	2,533 ft	Length:	8.3 mi
Top elevation:	11,992 ft	Average grade:	5.8%
Minimum grade:	2%	Maximum grade:	9%
Distance ≥ 5%:	5.6 miles	Distance ≥ 10%:	0.0 mi
Steepest mile:	6.4%	Steepest 3 miles:	6.2%
Traffic:	2	Descent:	3

Mount Evans

Total elevation:	6,590 ft	Length:	27.8 mi
Top elevation:	14,130 ft	Average grade:	4.5%
Minimum grade:	0%	Maximum grade:	10%
Distance ≥ 5%:	9.8 miles	Distance ≥ 10%:	0.0 mi
Steepest mile:	6.8%	Steepest 3 miles:	5.8%
Traffic:	2	Descent:	4

Guanella Pass

Total elevation:	1,590 ft	Length:	5.8 mi
Top elevation:	10,109 ft	Average grade:	5.2%
Minimum grade:	0%	Maximum grade:	10%
Distance ≥ 5%:	3.4 miles	Distance ≥ 10%:	0.1 mi
Steepest mile:	6.1%	Steepest 3 miles:	5.8%
Traffic:	1	Descent:	4

Juniper Pass East

Total elevation:	3,353 ft	Length:	16.0 mi
Top elevation:	11,130 ft	Average grade:	4.0%
Minimum grade:	3%	Maximum grade:	6%
Distance ≥ 5%:	4.9 miles	Distance ≥ 10%:	0.0 mi
Steepest mile:	5.5%	Steepest 3 miles:	4.9%
Traffic:	1	Descent:	3

Juniper Pass West

Total elevation:	3,590 ft	Length:	15.9 mi
Top elevation:	11,130 ft	Average grade:	4.5%
Minimum grade:	0%	Maximum grade:	7%
Distance ≥ 5%:	5.8 miles	Distance ≥ 10%:	0.0 mi
Steepest mile:	6.4%	Steepest 3 miles:	5.8%
Traffic:	2	Descent:	3

South Turkey Creek Road

Total elevation:	1,075 ft	Length:	7.9 mi
Top elevation:	7,856 ft	Average grade:	2.6%
Minimum grade:	0%	Maximum grade:	8%
Distance ≥ 5%:	2.2 miles	Distance ≥ 10%:	0.0 mi
Steepest mile:	5.8%	Steepest 3 miles:	5.2%
Traffic:	2	Descent:	3

Deer Creek Canyon Road

Total elevation:	1,624 ft	Length:	7.1 mi
Top elevation:	7,257 ft	Average grade:	4.3%
Minimum grade:	0%	Maximum grade:	9%
Distance ≥ 5%:	3.2 miles	Distance ≥ 10%:	0.0 mi
Steepest mile:	6.3%	Steepest 3 miles:	5.9%
Traffic:	2	Descent:	3

South Deer Creek Canyon

Total elevation:	2,777 ft	Length:	11.3 mi
Top elevation:	8,410 ft	Average grade:	4.7%
Minimum grade:	1%	Maximum grade:	8%
Distance ≥ 5%:	3.7 miles	Distance ≥ 10%:	0.0 mi
Steepest mile:	5.9%	Steepest 3 miles:	5.5%
Traffic:	1	Descent:	3

Kenosha Pass East

Total elevation:	2,212 ft	Length:	18.6 mi
Top elevation:	9,994 ft	Average grade:	2.3%
Minimum grade:	0%	Maximum grade:	7%
Distance ≥ 5%:	1.9 miles	Distance ≥ 10%:	0.0 mi
Steepest mile:	4.9%	Steepest 3 miles:	4.7%
Traffic:	3	Descent:	2

Cottonwood Pass

Total elevation:	3,597 ft	Length:	13.5 mi
Top elevation:	12,126 ft	Average grade:	5.0%
Minimum grade:	0%	Maximum grade:	10%
Distance ≥ 5%:	9.9 miles	Distance ≥ 10%:	0.0 mi
Steepest mile:	6.1%	Steepest 3 miles:	5.7%
Traffic:	2	Descent:	4

Trout Creek Pass West

Total elevation:	1,606 ft	Length:	11.8 mi
Top elevation:	9,487 ft	Average grade:	2.6%
Minimum grade:	0%	Maximum grade:	5%
Distance ≥ 5%:	1.4 miles	Distance ≥ 10%:	0.0 mi
Steepest mile:	4.5%	Steepest 3 miles:	3.8%
Traffic:	3	Descent:	3

Wilkerson Pass East

Total elevation:	1,625 ft	Length:	9.8 mi
Top elevation:	9,507 ft	Average grade:	3.1%
Minimum grade:	3%	Maximum grade:	6%
Distance ≥ 5%:	2.2 miles	Distance ≥ 10%:	0.0 mi
Steepest mile:	5.1%	Steepest 3 miles:	4.3%
Traffic:	2	Descent:	3

Ute Pass East

Total elevation:	2,937 ft	Length:	21.1 mi
Top elevation:	9,165 ft	Average grade:	2.6%
Minimum grade:	0%	Maximum grade:	6%
Distance ≥ 5%:	3.5 miles	Distance ≥ 10%:	0.0 mi
Steepest mile:	5.5%	Steepest 3 miles:	5.2%
Traffic:	3	Descent:	3

Ute Pass West

Total elevation:	1,011 ft	Length:	8.5 mi
Top elevation:	9,165 ft	Average grade:	2.3%
Minimum grade:	0%	Maximum grade:	5%
Distance ≥ 5%:	6.9 miles	Distance ≥ 10%:	0.0 mi
Steepest mile:	4.2%	Steepest 3 miles:	3.8%
Traffic:	2	Descent:	3

Pikes Peak

Total elevation:	3,796 ft	Length:	15.7 mi
Top elevation:	10,024 ft	Average grade:	4.6%
Minimum grade:	0%	Maximum grade:	10%
Distance ≥ 5%:	7.8 miles	Distance ≥ 10%:	0.2 mi
Steepest mile:	9.2%	Steepest 3 miles:	5.9%
Traffic:	2	Descent:	3

Cheyenne Mountain

Total elevation:	1,228 ft	Length:	3.3 mi
Top elevation:	7,505 ft	Average grade:	7.0%
Minimum grade:	1%	Maximum grade:	12%
Distance ≥ 5%:	2.7 miles	Distance ≥ 10%:	0.3 mi
Steepest mile:	7.6%	Steepest 3 miles:	7.1%
Traffic:	2	Descent:	4

Gold Camp Road

Total elevation:	841 ft	Length:	4.4 mi
Top elevation:	7,084 ft	Average grade:	3.6%
Minimum grade:	3%	Maximum grade:	10%
Distance ≥ 5%:	5.9 miles	Distance ≥ 10%:	0.0 mi
Steepest mile:	4.7%	Steepest 3 miles:	3.7%
Traffic:	2	Descent:	3

Poncha Pass North

Total elevation:	1,558 ft	Length:	6.9 mi
Top elevation:	9,019 ft	Average grade:	4.3%
Minimum grade:	1%	Maximum grade:	7%
Distance ≥ 5%:	1.5 miles	Distance ≥ 10%:	0.0 mi
Steepest mile:	5.7%	Steepest 3 miles:	4.7%
Traffic:	2	Descent:	3

96 East

Total elevation:	2,947 ft	Length:	13.8 mi
Top elevation:	9,056 ft	Average grade:	4.0%
Minimum grade:	0%	Maximum grade:	7%
Distance ≥ 5%:	5.6 miles	Distance ≥ 10%:	0.0 mi
Steepest mile:	5.8%	Steepest 3 miles:	5.1%
Traffic:	2	Descent:	3

Hardscrabble Pass West

Total elevation:	1,090 ft	Length:	9.9 mi
Top elevation:	9,085 ft	Average grade:	2.1%
Minimum grade:	0%	Maximum grade:	6%
Distance ≥ 5%:	2.8 miles	Distance ≥ 10%:	0.0 mi
Steepest mile:	4.7%	Steepest 3 miles:	4.2%
Traffic:	2	Descent:	2

96/165

Total elevation:	3,286 ft	Length:	14.1 mi
Top elevation:	9,395 ft	Average grade:	4.4%
Minimum grade:	0%	Maximum grade:	7%
Distance ≥ 5%:	5.6 miles	Distance ≥ 10%:	0.0 mi
Steepest mile:	5.9%	Steepest 3 miles:	5.1%
Traffic:	1	Descent:	3

165 South

Total elevation:	2,633 ft	Length:	13.6 mi
Top elevation:	9,352 ft	Average grade:	3.7%
Minimum grade:	0%	Maximum grade:	7%
Distance ≥ 5%:	6.3 miles	Distance ≥ 10%:	0.0 mi
Steepest mile:	5.5%	Steepest 3 miles:	4.9%
Traffic:	1	Descent:	3

North La Veta Pass East

Total elevation:	1,926 ft	Length:	8.2 mi
Top elevation:	9,413 ft	Average grade:	4.4%
Minimum grade:	1%	Maximum grade:	7%
Distance ≥ 5%:	2.7 miles	Distance ≥ 10%:	0.0 mi
Steepest mile:	5.4%	Steepest 3 miles:	4.8%
Traffic:	3	Descent:	1

North La Veta Pass West

Total elevation:	1,135 ft	Length:	8.4 mi
Top elevation:	9,413 ft	Average grade:	2.6%
Minimum grade:	0%	Maximum grade:	5%
Distance ≥ 5%:	1.7 miles	Distance ≥ 10%:	0.0 mi
Steepest mile:	4.1%	Steepest 3 miles:	3.6%
Traffic:	3	Descent:	2

Cucharas Pass North

Total elevation:	2,411 ft	Length:	16.3 mi
Top elevation:	9,941 ft	Average grade:	2.8%
Minimum grade:	0%	Maximum grade:	7%
Distance ≥ 5%:	4.8 miles	Distance ≥ 10%:	0.0 mi
Steepest mile:	6.2%	Steepest 3 miles:	5.6%
Traffic:	1	Descent:	3

On the way to the top of Route 96

Views from North La Veta Pass

Cucharas Pass South

Total elevation:	**2,135 ft**	**Length:**	**15.2 mi**
Top elevation:	**1,659 ft**	**Average grade:**	**2.7%**
Minimum grade:	**0%**	**Maximum grade:**	**8%**
Distance ≥ 5%:	**4.2 miles**	**Distance ≥ 10%:**	**0.0 mi**
Steepest mile:	**7.5%**	**Steepest 3 miles:**	**4.5%**
Traffic:	**1**	**Descent:**	**3**

Steep Colorado grade

Western Colorado

Belly Ache

Total elevation:	2,066 ft	Length:	5.2 mi
Top elevation:	9,074 ft	Average grade:	7.5%
Minimum grade:	2%	Maximum grade:	10%
Distance ≥ 5%:	3.9 miles	Distance ≥ 10%:	0.2 mi
Steepest mile:	7.8%	Steepest 3 miles:	7.7%
Traffic:	1	Descent:	4

Squaw Creek Road

Total elevation:	1,094 ft	Length:	4.1 mi
Top elevation:	8,203 ft	Average grade:	5.1%
Minimum grade:	1%	Maximum grade:	10%
Distance ≥ 5%:	2.4 miles	Distance ≥ 10%:	0.1 mi
Steepest mile:	6.9%	Steepest 3 miles:	5.6%
Traffic:	2	Descent:	3

Douglas Pass North

Total elevation:	1,173 ft	Length:	3.1 mi
Top elevation:	8,268 ft	Average grade:	7.2%
Minimum grade:	0%	Maximum grade:	8%
Distance ≥ 5%:	2.7 miles	Distance ≥ 10%:	0.0 mi
Steepest mile:	7.4%	Steepest 3 miles:	7.3%
Traffic:	2	Descent:	3

Douglas Pass South

Total elevation:	1,467 ft	Length:	4.2 mi
Top elevation:	8,268 ft	Average grade:	6.6%
Minimum grade:	3%	Maximum grade:	8%
Distance ≥ 5%:	3.3 miles	Distance ≥ 10%:	0.0 mi
Steepest mile:	6.9%	Steepest 3 miles:	6.7%
Traffic:	2	Descent:	4

Colorado National Monument East

Total elevation:	1,902 ft	Length:	8.4 mi
Top elevation:	6,503 ft	Average grade:	4.3%
Minimum grade:	1%	Maximum grade:	9%
Distance ≥ 5%:	3.1 miles	Distance ≥ 10%:	0.0 mi
Steepest mile:	5.8%	Steepest 3 miles:	5.5%
Traffic:	2	Descent:	4

The south side of Douglas Pass

Scenic Colorado National Monument

Colorado National Monument West

Total elevation:	1,352 ft	Length:	5.8 mi
Top elevation:	5,851 ft	Average grade:	4.4%
Minimum grade:	1%	Maximum grade:	8%
Distance ≥ 5%:	2.6 miles	Distance ≥ 10%:	0.0 mi
Steepest mile:	6.2%	Steepest 3 miles:	5.2%
Traffic:	2	Descent:	4

141 East

Total elevation:	1,213 ft	Length:	6.5 mi
Top elevation:	6,006 ft	Average grade:	3.9%
Minimum grade:	0%	Maximum grade:	6%
Distance ≥ 5%:	2.3 miles	Distance ≥ 10%:	0.0 mi
Steepest mile:	4.6%	Steepest 3 miles:	4.4%
Traffic:	2	Descent:	3

Lands End

Total elevation:	1,624 ft	Length:	9.0 mi
Top elevation:	6,466 ft	Average grade:	3.4%
Minimum grade:	1%	Maximum grade:	8%
Distance ≥ 5%:	3.4 miles	Distance ≥ 10%:	0.0 mi
Steepest mile:	5.6%	Steepest 3 miles:	5.2%
Traffic:	1	Descent:	2

Bonham Reservoir

Total elevation:	2,193 ft	Length:	7.3 mi
Top elevation:	8,204 ft	Average grade:	5.7%
Minimum grade:	0%	Maximum grade:	9%
Distance ≥ 5%:	5.5 miles	Distance ≥ 10%:	0.0 mi
Steepest mile:	6.7%	Steepest 3 miles:	6.3%
Traffic:	1	Descent:	2

Grand Mesa North

Total elevation:	5,622 ft	Length:	21.4 mi
Top elevation:	10,852 ft	Average grade:	5.0%
Minimum grade:	0%	Maximum grade:	7%
Distance ≥ 5%:	13.8 miles	Distance ≥ 10%:	0.0 mi
Steepest mile:	6.0%	Steepest 3 miles:	5.8%
Traffic:	1	Descent:	3

Grand Mesa South

Total elevation:	4,752 ft	Length:	20.7 mi
Top elevation:	10,852 ft	Average grade:	4.3%
Minimum grade:	0%	Maximum grade:	6%
Distance ≥ 5%:	8.8 miles	Distance ≥ 10%:	0.0 mi
Steepest mile:	5.4%	Steepest 3 miles:	5.1%
Traffic:	1	Descent:	3

McClure Pass East

Total elevation:	1,268 ft	Length:	4.2 mi
Top elevation:	8,780 ft	Average grade:	5.7%
Minimum grade:	1%	Maximum grade:	9%
Distance ≥ 5%:	3.1 miles	Distance ≥ 10%:	0.0 mi
Steepest mile:	7.0%	Steepest 3 miles:	6.8%
Traffic:	2	Descent:	3

McClure Pass West

Total elevation:	1,914 ft	Length:	7.7 mi
Top elevation:	8,780 ft	Average grade:	4.7%
Minimum grade:	0%	Maximum grade:	7%
Distance ≥ 5%:	3.6 miles	Distance ≥ 10%:	0.0 mi
Steepest mile:	6.1%	Steepest 3 miles:	5.8%
Traffic:	2	Descent:	3

Independence Pass East

Total elevation:	2,870 ft	Length:	17.4 mi
Top elevation:	12,095 ft	Average grade:	3.1%
Minimum grade:	0%	Maximum grade:	6%
Distance ≥ 5%:	6.7 miles	Distance ≥ 10%:	0.0 mi
Steepest mile:	5.6%	Steepest 3 miles:	5.5%
Traffic:	2	Descent:	3

Independence Pass West

Total elevation:	3,991 ft	Length:	15.9 mi
Top elevation:	12,095 ft	Average grade:	4.8%
Minimum grade:	0%	Maximum grade:	7%
Distance ≥ 5%:	9.4 miles	Distance ≥ 10%:	0.0 mi
Steepest mile:	6.3%	Steepest 3 miles:	6.0%
Traffic:	2	Descent:	4

East Portal

Total elevation:	1,938 ft	Length:	3.0 mi
Top elevation:	8,455 ft	Average grade:	12.2%
Minimum grade:	1%	Maximum grade:	16%
Distance ≥ 5%:	2.8 miles	Distance ≥ 10%:	2.6 mi
Steepest mile:	13.5%	Steepest 3 miles:	12.2%
Traffic:	1	Descent:	5

Monarch Pass East

Total elevation:	3,177 ft	Length:	11.5 mi
Top elevation:	11,312 ft	Average grade:	5.2%
Minimum grade:	1%	Maximum grade:	7%
Distance ≥ 5%:	6.6 miles	Distance ≥ 10%:	0.0 mi
Steepest mile:	6.6%	Steepest 3 miles:	6.3%
Traffic:	2	Descent:	2

Monarch Pass West

Total elevation:	2,850 ft	Length:	9.9 mi
Top elevation:	11,312 ft	Average grade:	5.5%
Minimum grade:	2%	Maximum grade:	7%
Distance ≥ 5%:	8.4 miles	Distance ≥ 10%:	0.0 mi
Steepest mile:	6.6%	Steepest 3 miles:	6.2%
Traffic:	2	Descent:	2

North Pass East

Total elevation:	1,425 ft	Length:	5.7 mi
Top elevation:	10,149 ft	Average grade:	4.7%
Minimum grade:	1%	Maximum grade:	7%
Distance ≥ 5%:	4.1 miles	Distance ≥ 10%:	0.0 mi
Steepest mile:	5.3%	Steepest 3 miles:	5.0%
Traffic:	1	Descent:	3

North Pass West

Total elevation:	1,171 ft	Length:	10.8 mi
Top elevation:	10,149 ft	Average grade:	2.1%
Minimum grade:	0%	Maximum grade:	7%
Distance ≥ 5%:	3.4 miles	Distance ≥ 10%:	0.0 mi
Steepest mile:	6.7%	Steepest 3 miles:	4.7%
Traffic:	1	Descent:	3

Dallas Divide East

Total elevation:	1,968 ft	Length:	10.3 mi
Top elevation:	8,970 ft	Average grade:	3.6%
Minimum grade:	0%	Maximum grade:	7%
Distance ≥ 5%:	3.2 miles	Distance ≥ 10%:	0.0 mi
Steepest mile:	5.8%	Steepest 3 miles:	5.2%
Traffic:	2	Descent:	3

Dallas Divide West

Total elevation:	1,659 ft	Length:	12.3 mi
Top elevation:	8,970 ft	Average grade:	2.6%
Minimum grade:	0%	Maximum grade:	5%
Distance ≥ 5%:	2.5 miles	Distance ≥ 10%:	0.0 mi
Steepest mile:	5.0%	Steepest 3 miles:	4.3%
Traffic:	1	Descent:	3

Lizard Head Pass North

Total elevation:	1,552 ft	Length:	11.7 mi
Top elevation:	10,250 ft	Average grade:	2.5%
Minimum grade:	0%	Maximum grade:	6%
Distance ≥ 5%:	3.6 miles	Distance ≥ 10%:	0.0 mi
Steepest mile:	5.8%	Steepest 3 miles:	5.4%
Traffic:	1	Descent:	4

Lizard Head Pass South

Total elevation:	1,423 ft	Length:	11.6 mi
Top elevation:	10,250 ft	Average grade:	2.3%
Minimum grade:	0%	Maximum grade:	7%
Distance ≥ 5%:	2.7 miles	Distance ≥ 10%:	0.0 mi
Steepest mile:	6.7%	Steepest 3 miles:	4.1%
Traffic:	2	Descent:	3

Mesa Verde National Park

Total elevation:	972 ft	Length:	3.5 mi
Top elevation:	7,937 ft	Average grade:	5.3%
Minimum grade:	2%	Maximum grade:	7%
Distance ≥ 5%:	1.9 miles	Distance ≥ 10%:	0.0 mi
Steepest mile:	5.6%	Steepest 3 miles:	5.4%
Traffic:	1	Descent:	3

160 East

Total elevation:	1,709 ft	Length:	7.6 mi
Top elevation:	8,221ft	Average grade:	4.3%
Minimum grade:	0%	Maximum grade:	6%
Distance ≥ 5%:	2.9 miles	Distance ≥ 10%:	0.0 mi
Steepest mile:	5.2%	Steepest 3 miles:	4.6%
Traffic:	3	Descent:	3

The climb up Mesa Verde

A rider struggles on NCAR

Red Mountain Pass North

Total elevation:	3,200 ft	Length:	12.5 mi
Top elevation:	11,018 ft	Average grade:	4.8%
Minimum grade:	2%	Maximum grade:	8%
Distance ≥ 5%:	6.8 miles	Distance ≥ 10%:	0.0 mi
Steepest mile:	6.7%	Steepest 3 miles:	6.2%
Traffic:	2	Descent:	4

Red Mountain Pass South

Total elevation:	1,702 ft	Length:	9.8 mi
Top elevation:	11,018 ft	Average grade:	3.3%
Minimum grade:	0%	Maximum grade:	7%
Distance ≥ 5%:	3.7 miles	Distance ≥ 10%:	0.0 mi
Steepest mile:	6.5%	Steepest 3 miles:	5.9%
Traffic:	2	Descent:	3

Molas Pass North

Total elevation:	1,671 ft	Length:	6.3 mi
Top elevation:	10,910 ft	Average grade:	5.0%
Minimum grade:	2%	Maximum grade:	7%
Distance ≥ 5%:	3.2 miles	Distance ≥ 10%:	0.0 mi
Steepest mile:	6.1%	Steepest 3 miles:	5.6%
Traffic:	2	Descent:	3

Views from Red Mountain

The top of Molas Pass

Molas Pass South

Total elevation:	1,123 ft	Length:	4.2 mi
Top elevation:	10,910 ft	Average grade:	5.1%
Minimum grade:	2%	Maximum grade:	7%
Distance ≥ 5%:	2.3 miles	Distance ≥ 10%:	0.0 mi
Steepest mile:	6.0%	Steepest 3 miles:	5.3%
Traffic:	2	Descent:	3

Coal Bank Pass North

Total elevation:	843 ft	Length:	2.8 mi
Top elevation:	10,630 ft	Average grade:	5.7%
Minimum grade:	2%	Maximum grade:	7%
Distance ≥ 5%:	2.5 miles	Distance ≥ 10%:	0.0 mi
Steepest mile:	6.1%	Steepest 3 miles:	NA
Traffic:	2	Descent:	3

Coal Bank Pass South

Total elevation:	3,831 ft	Length:	20.1 mi
Top elevation:	10,630 ft	Average grade:	3.6%
Minimum grade:	0%	Maximum grade:	8%
Distance ≥ 5%:	6.9 miles	Distance ≥ 10%:	0.0 mi
Steepest mile:	7.6%	Steepest 3 miles:	6.8%
Traffic:	2	Descent:	3

Slumgullion Pass East

Total elevation:	1,084 ft	Length:	4.3 mi
Top elevation:	11,530 ft	Average grade:	4.8%
Minimum grade:	2%	Maximum grade:	5%
Distance ≥ 5%:	1.1 miles	Distance ≥ 10%:	0.0 mi
Steepest mile:	5.0%	Steepest 3 miles:	4.8%
Traffic:	1	Descent:	3

Slumgullion Pass West

Total elevation:	2,476 ft	Length:	7.7 mi
Top elevation:	11,530 ft	Average grade:	6.1%
Minimum grade:	2%	Maximum grade:	9%
Distance ≥ 5%:	5.9 miles	Distance ≥ 10%:	0.0 mi
Steepest mile:	7.4%	Steepest 3 miles:	7.1%
Traffic:	1	Descent:	4

Wolf Creek Pass North

Total elevation:	2,271 ft	Length:	9.4 mi
Top elevation:	10,850 ft	Average grade:	4.6%
Minimum grade:	3%	Maximum grade:	7%
Distance ≥ 5%:	4.6 miles	Distance ≥ 10%:	0.0 mi
Steepest mile:	6.6%	Steepest 3 miles:	6.4%
Traffic:	2	Descent:	3

Wolf Creek Pass South

Total elevation:	2,943 ft	Length:	8.5 mi
Top elevation:	10,850 ft	Average grade:	6.6%
Minimum grade:	4%	Maximum grade:	8%
Distance ≥ 5%:	7.2 miles	Distance ≥ 10%:	0.0 mi
Steepest mile:	6.8%	Steepest 3 miles:	6.7%
Traffic:	2	Descent:	2

Cumbres Pass South

Total elevation:	2,105 ft	Length:	11.2 mi
Top elevation:	10,022 ft	Average grade:	3.6%
Minimum grade:	0%	Maximum grade:	6%
Distance ≥ 5%:	2.3 miles	Distance ≥ 10%:	0.0 mi
Steepest mile:	4.9%	Steepest 3 miles:	4.7%
Traffic:	1	Descent:	2

La Manga Pass North

Total elevation:	1,393 ft	Length:	4.2 mi
Top elevation:	10,052 ft	Average grade:	6.3%
Minimum grade:	3%	Maximum grade:	8%
Distance ≥ 5%:	3.8 miles	Distance ≥ 10%:	0.0 mi
Steepest mile:	6.8%	Steepest 3 miles:	6.4%
Traffic:	1	Descent:	3

Increased grade on La Manga Pass

High elevation at Slumgullion Pass

Hill Climb Profiles (Top 25)
(in alphabetical order)

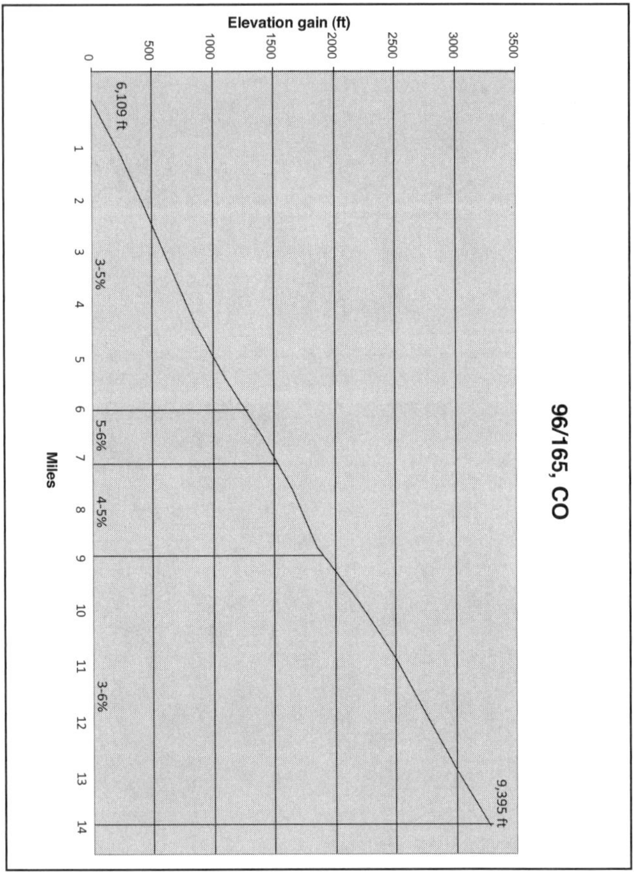

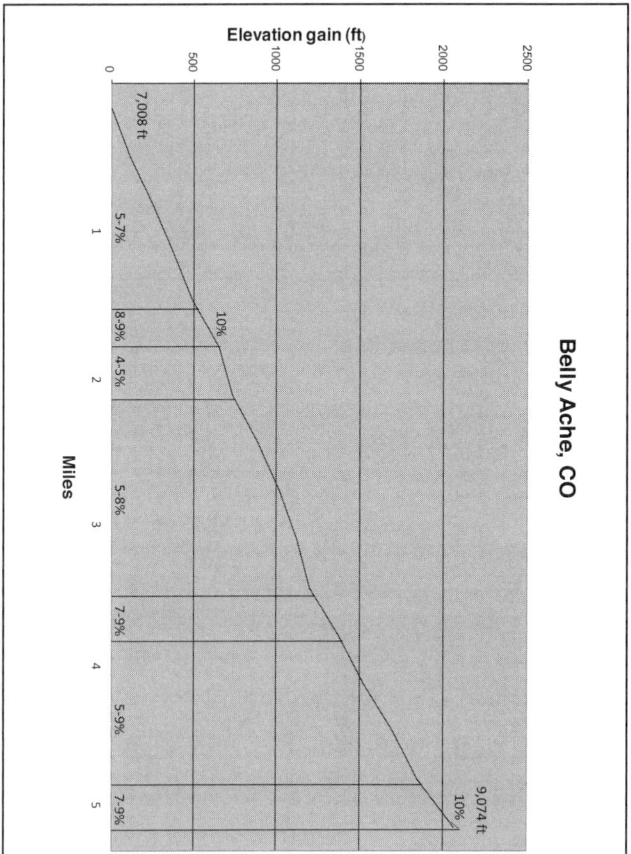
Belly Ache, CO
Elevation gain (ft)
0
500
1000
1500
2000
2500
Miles
1
2
3
4
5
7,008 ft
5-7%
8-9%
10%
4-5%
5-8%
7-9%
5-9%
7-9%
10%
9,074 ft

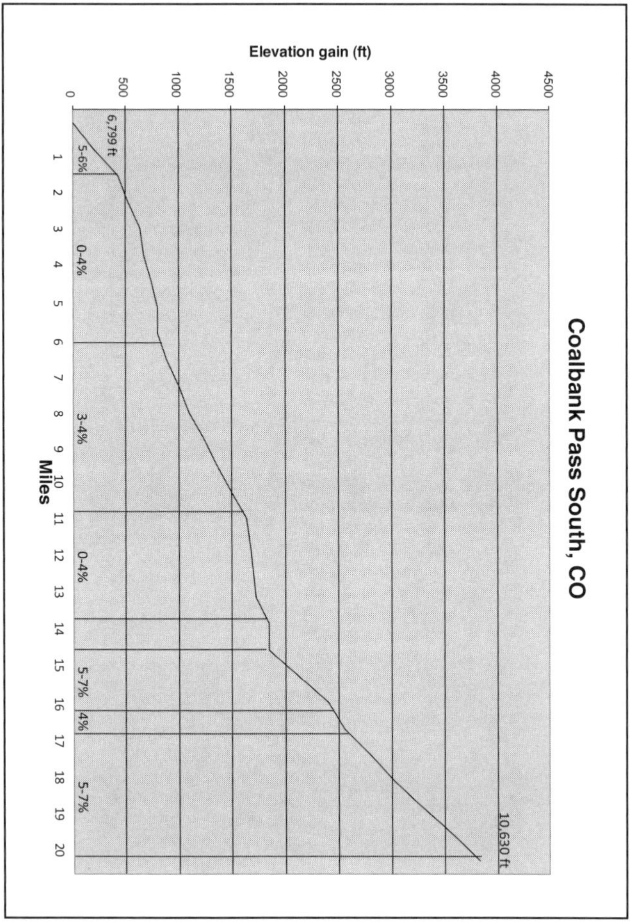

Coalbank Pass South, CO
Elevation gain (ft)
0
500
1000
1500
2000
2500
3000
3500
4000
4500
Miles
1
2
3
4
5
6
7
8
9
10
11
12
13
14
15
16
17
18
19
20
6,799 ft
5-6%
0-4%
3-4%
0-4%
5-7%
4%
5-7%
10,630 ft

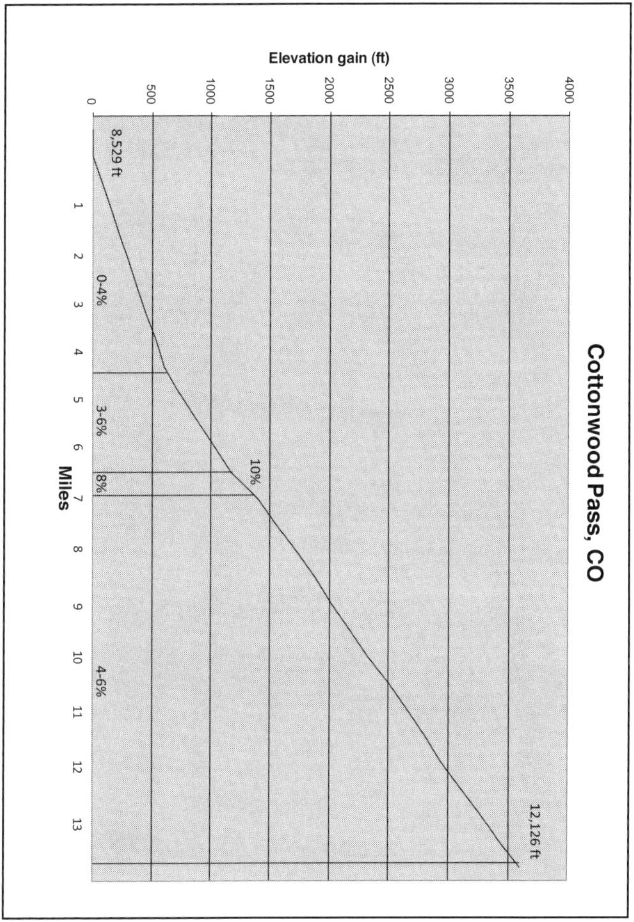
Cottonwood Pass, CO
Elevation gain (ft)
0
500
1000
1500
2000
2500
3000
3500
4000
8,529 ft
0-4%
3-6%
10%
8%
4-6%
12,126 ft
1
2
3
4
5
6
7
8
9
10
11
12
13
Miles

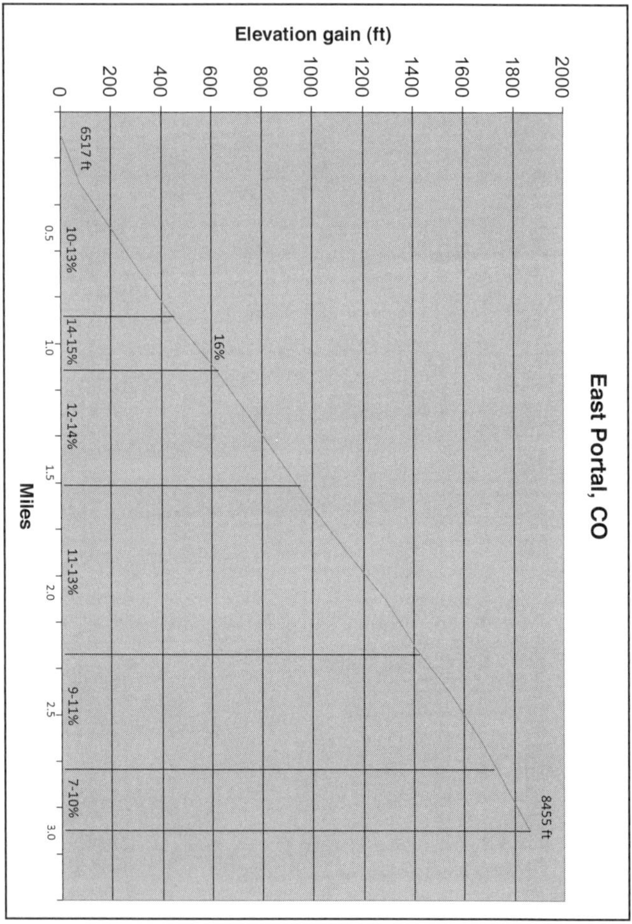
East Portal, CO
Elevation gain (ft)
0
200
400
600
800
1000
1200
1400
1600
1800
2000
6517 ft
10-13%
14-15%
16%
12-14%
11-13%
9-11%
7-10%
8455 ft
0.5
1.0
1.5
2.0
2.5
3.0
Miles

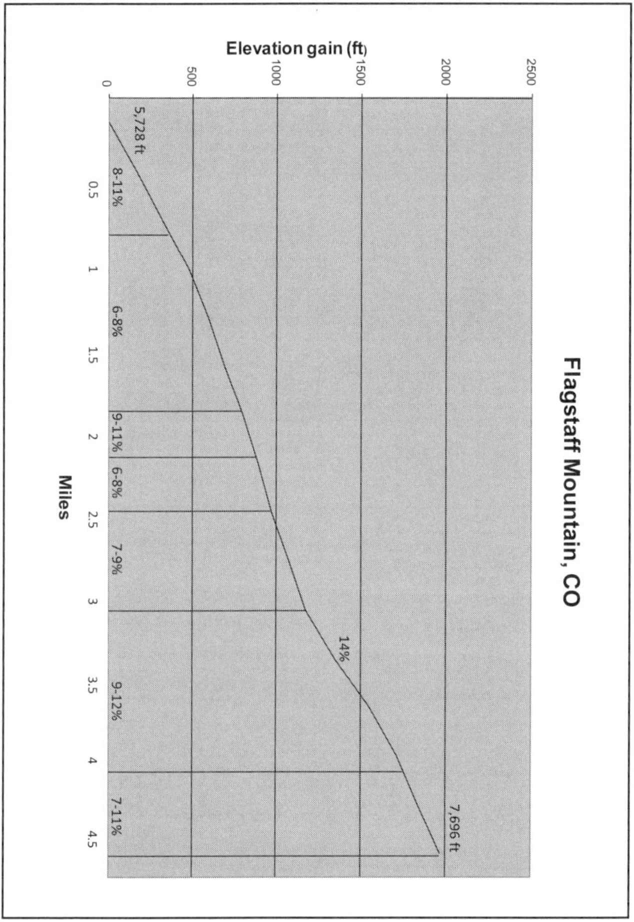
Flagstaff Mountain, CO
Elevation gain (ft)
0
500
1000
1500
2000
2500
5,728 ft
8-11%
6-8%
9-11%
6-8%
7-9%
14%
9-12%
7-11%
7,696 ft
0.5
1
1.5
2
2.5
3
3.5
4
4.5
Miles

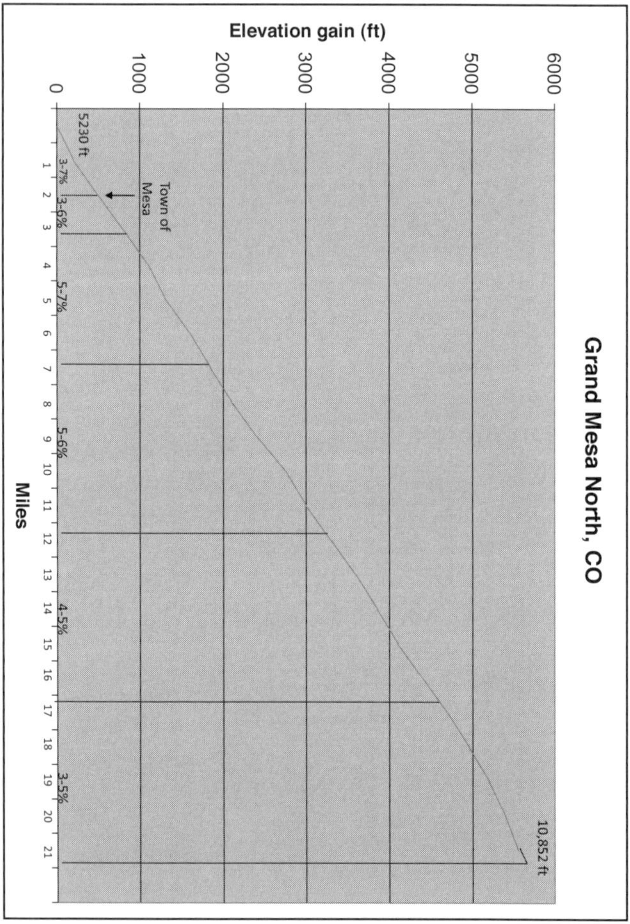
Grand Mesa North, CO
Elevation gain (ft)
0
1000
2000
3000
4000
5000
6000
Miles
1 2 3 4 5 6 7 8 9 10 11 12 13 14 15 16 17 18 19 20 21
5230 ft
10,852 ft
Town of Mesa
3-7%
3-6%
5-7%
5-6%
4-5%
3-5%

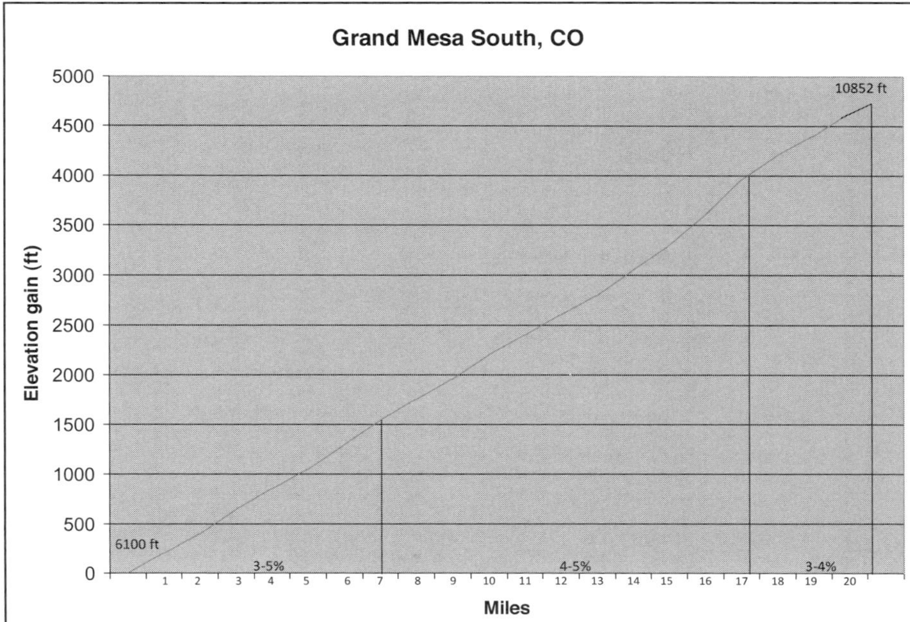
Grand Mesa South, CO
Elevation gain (ft)
5000
4500
4000
3500
3000
2500
2000
1500
1000
500
0
6100 ft
10852 ft
3-5%
4-5%
3-4%
1
2
3
4
5
6
7
8
9
10
11
12
13
14
15
16
17
18
19
20
Miles

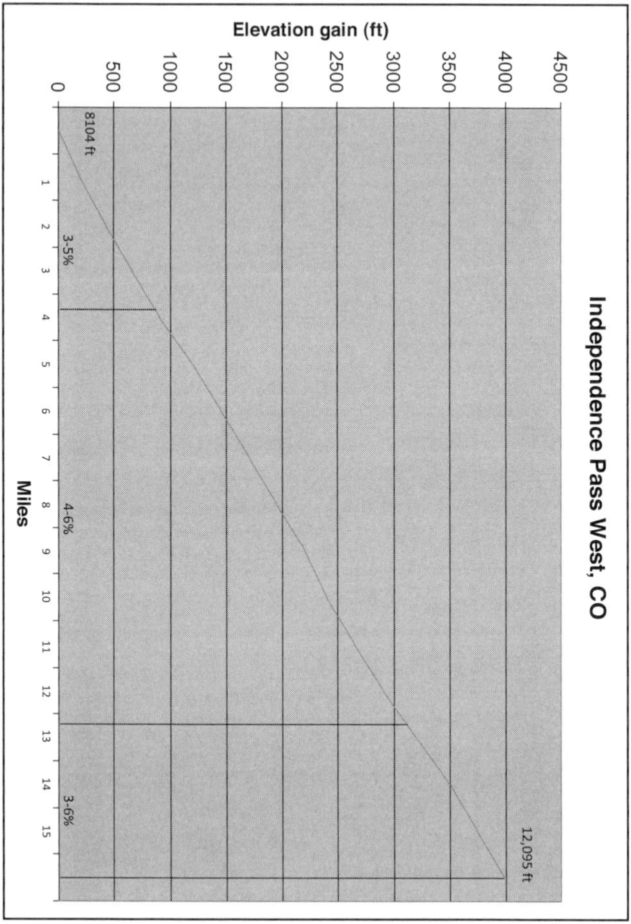

Independence Pass West, CO
Elevation gain (ft)
Miles
8104 ft
12,095 ft
3-5%
4-6%
3-6%

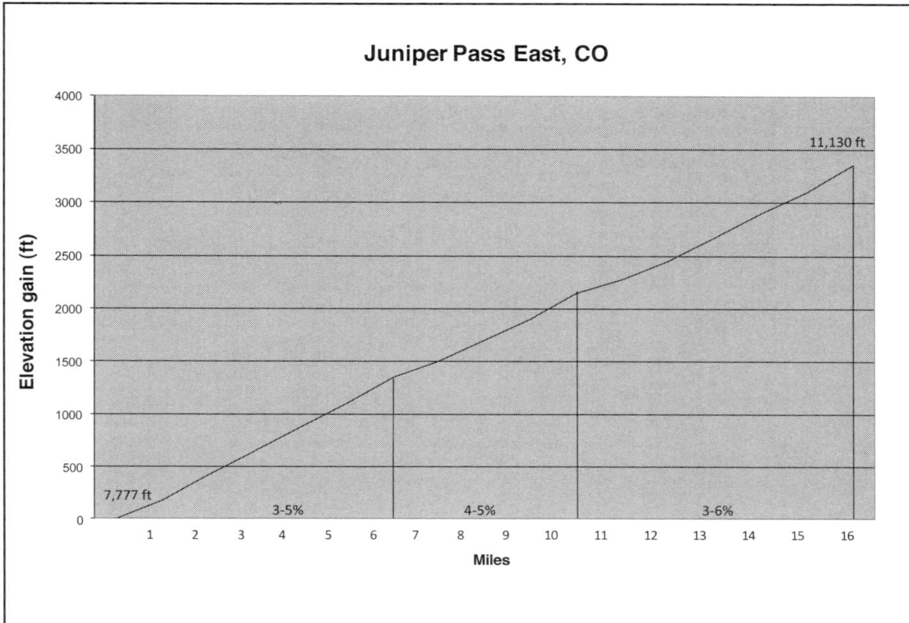
Juniper Pass East, CO
Elevation gain (ft)
0
500
1000
1500
2000
2500
3000
3500
4000
7,777 ft
11,130 ft
3-5%
4-5%
3-6%
1
2
3
4
5
6
7
8
9
10
11
12
13
14
15
16
Miles

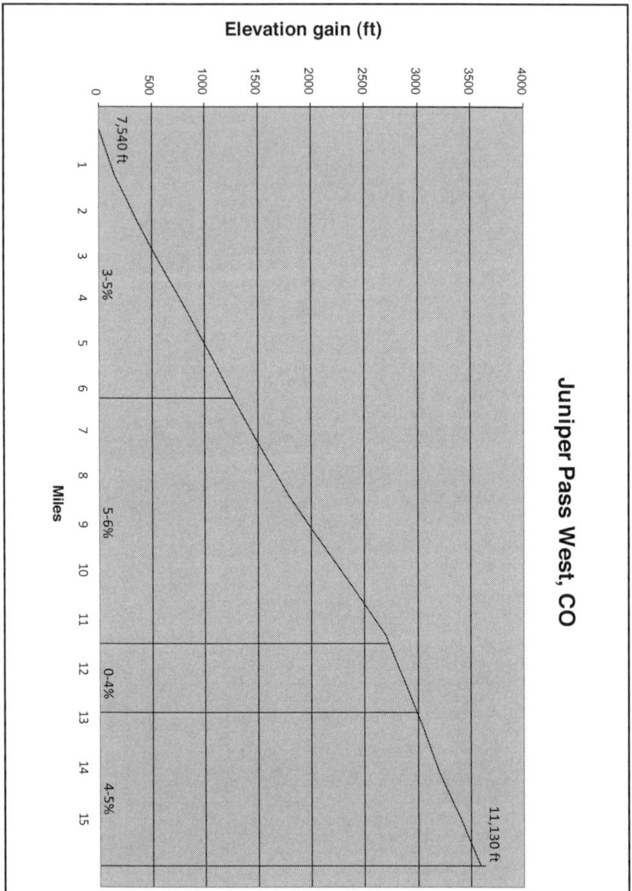

Juniper Pass West, CO
Elevation gain (ft)
0
500
1000
1500
2000
2500
3000
3500
4000
Miles
1
2
3
4
5
6
7
8
9
10
11
12
13
14
15
7,540 ft
3-5%
5-6%
0-4%
4-5%
11,130 ft

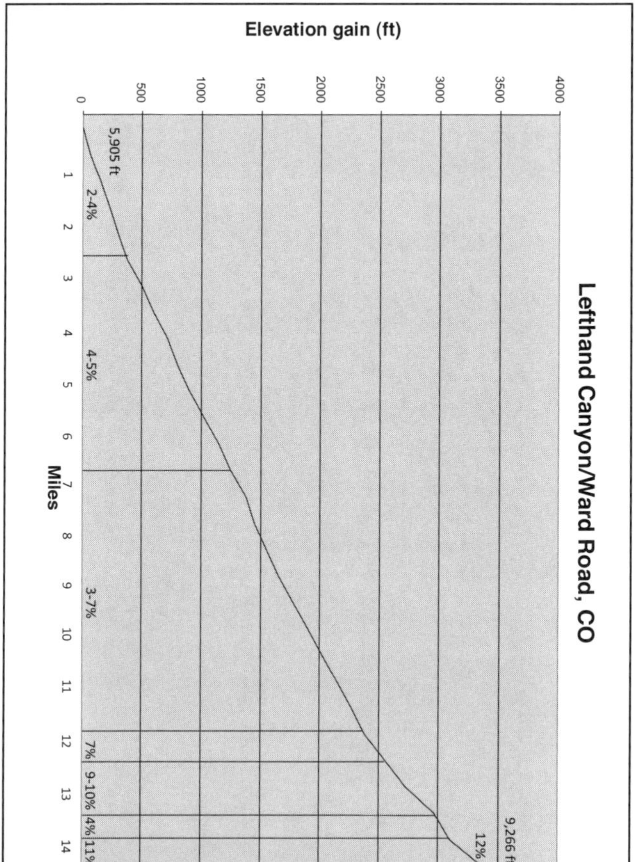
Lefthand Canyon/Ward Road, CO
Elevation gain (ft)
0
500
1000
1500
2000
2500
3000
3500
4000
Miles
1
2
3
4
5
6
7
8
9
10
11
12
13
14
5,905 ft
2-4%
4-5%
3-7%
7%
9-10%
4%
11%
12%
9,266 ft

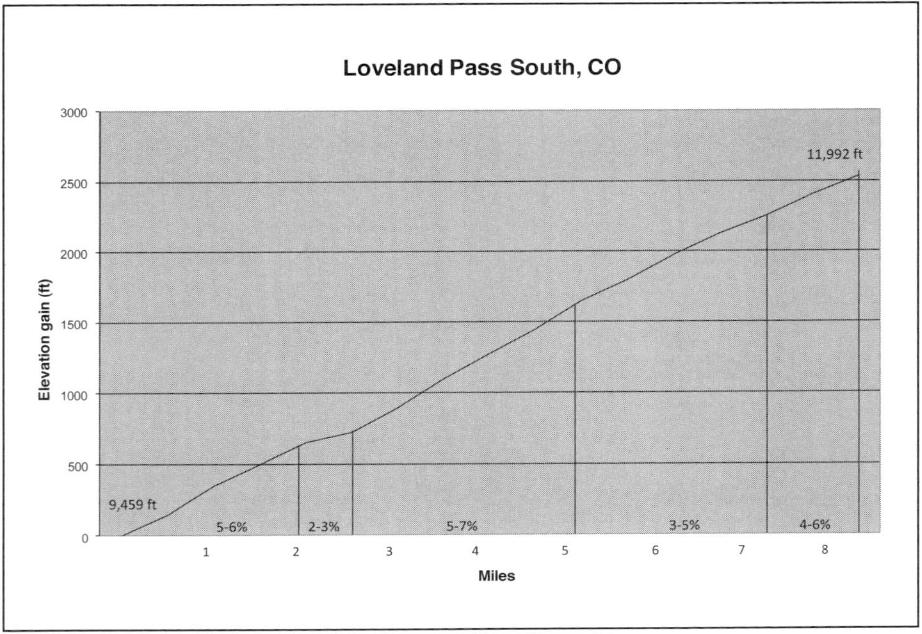

Loveland Pass South, CO
Elevation gain (ft)
3000
2500
2000
1500
1000
500
0
11,992 ft
9,459 ft
5-6%
2-3%
5-7%
3-5%
4-6%
1
2
3
4
5
6
7
8
Miles

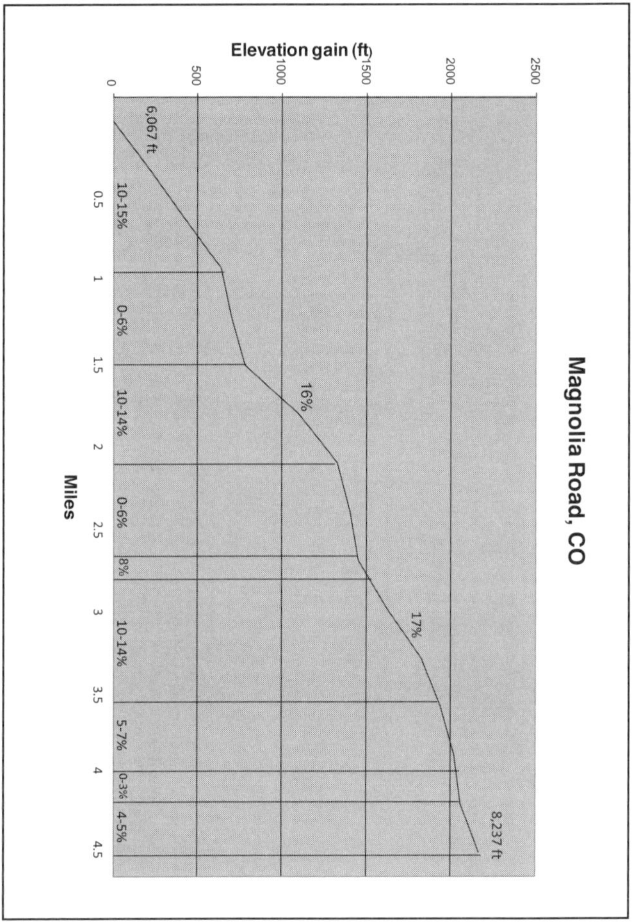
Magnolia Road, CO
Elevation gain (ft)
0
500
1000
1500
2000
2500
Miles
0.5
1
1.5
2
2.5
3
3.5
4
4.5
6,067 ft
8,237 ft
10-15%
0-6%
10-14%
16%
0-6%
8%
10-14%
17%
5-7%
0-3%
4-5%

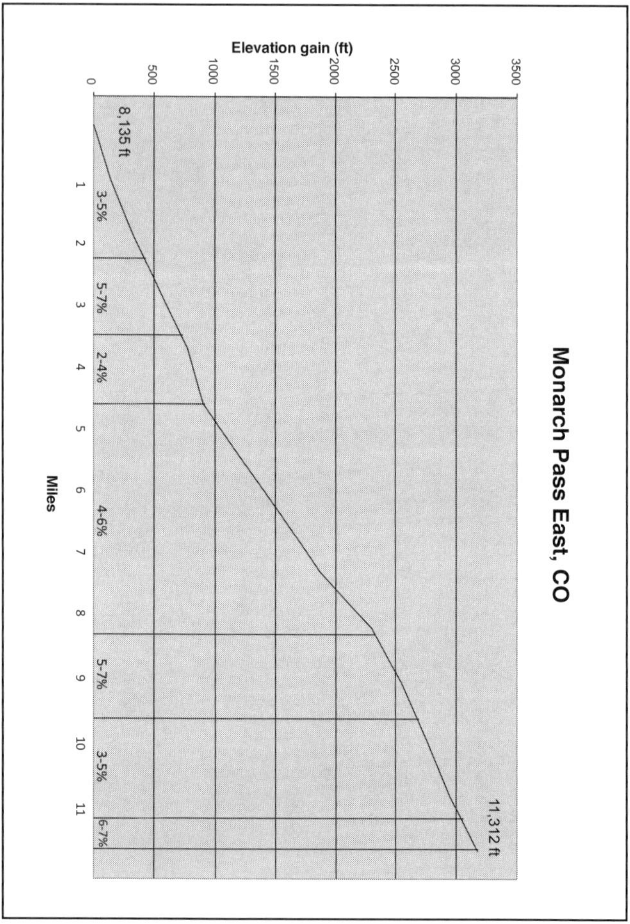
Monarch Pass East, CO
Elevation gain (ft)
0
500
1000
1500
2000
2500
3000
3500
Miles
1
2
3
4
5
6
7
8
9
10
11
8,135 ft
3-5%
5-7%
2-4%
4-6%
5-7%
3-5%
6-7%
11,312 ft

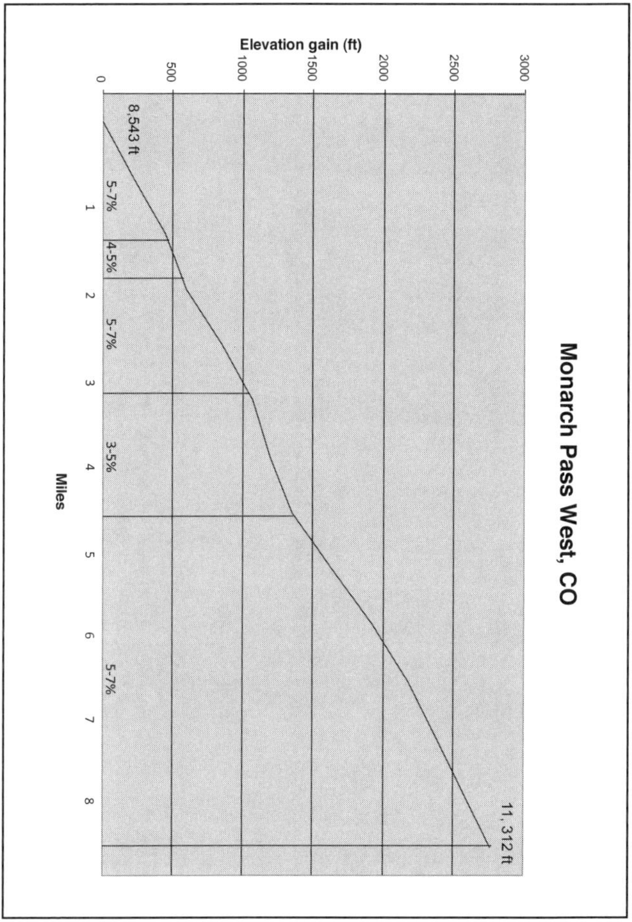
Monarch Pass West, CO
Elevation gain (ft)
0
500
1000
1500
2000
2500
3000
Miles
1
2
3
4
5
6
7
8
8,543 ft
5-7%
4-5%
5-7%
3-5%
5-7%
11, 312 ft

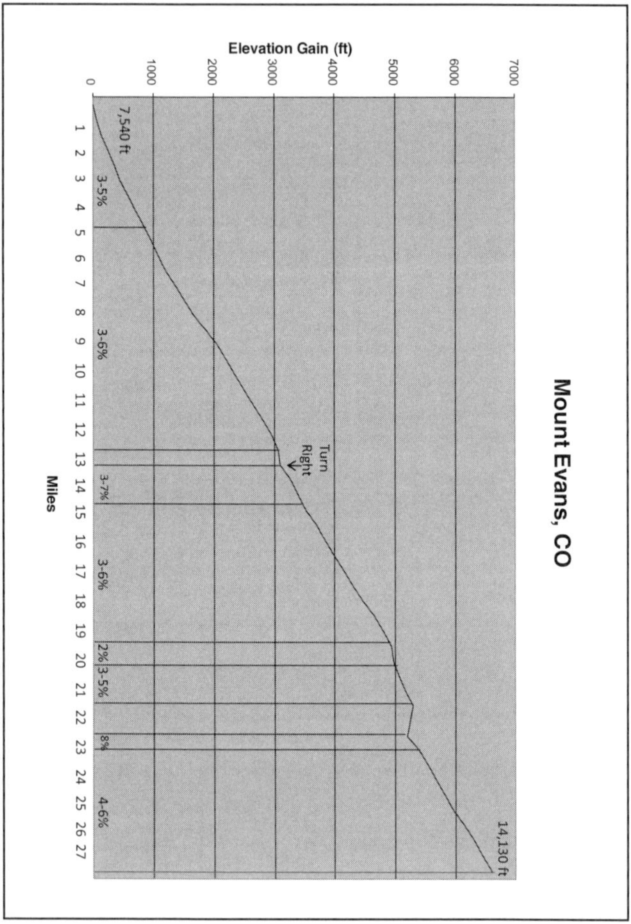
Mount Evans, CO
Elevation Gain (ft)
0
1000
2000
3000
4000
5000
6000
7000
Miles
1 2 3 4 5 6 7 8 9 10 11 12 13 14 15 16 17 18 19 20 21 22 23 24 25 26 27
7,540 ft
3-5%
3-6%
Turn Right
3-7%
3-6%
2%
3-5%
8%
4-6%
14,130 ft

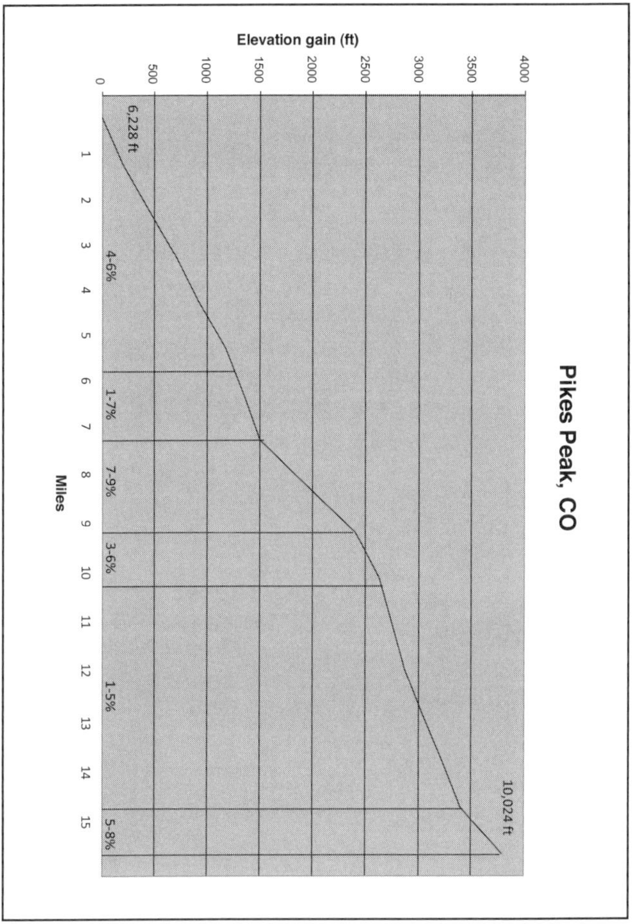
Pikes Peak, CO
Elevation gain (ft)
0
500
1000
1500
2000
2500
3000
3500
4000
Miles
1
2
3
4
5
6
7
8
9
10
11
12
13
14
15
6,228 ft
10,024 ft
4-6%
1-7%
7-9%
3-6%
1-5%
5-8%

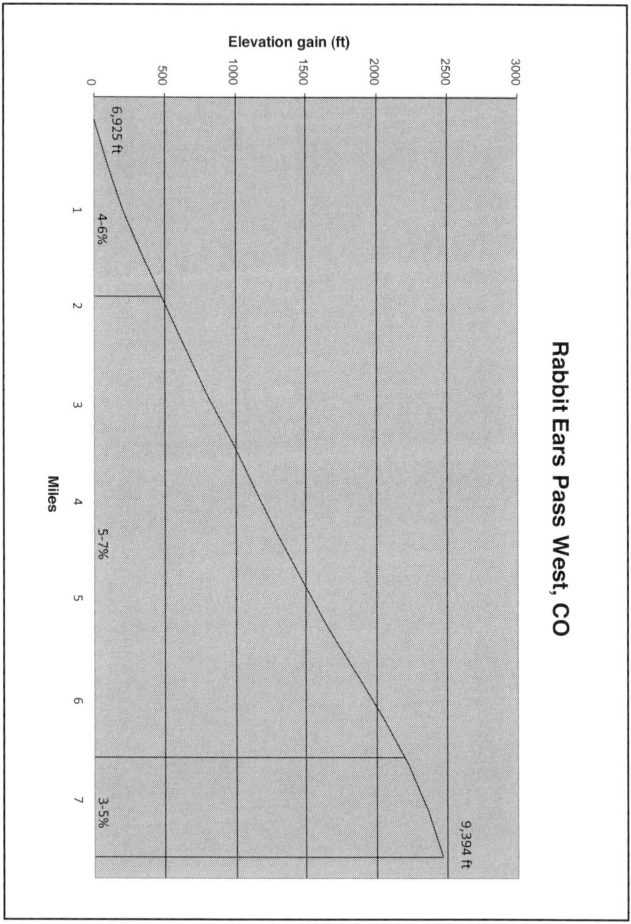

Rabbit Ears Pass West, CO
Elevation gain (ft)
0
500
1000
1500
2000
2500
3000
Miles
1
2
3
4
5
6
7
6,925 ft
4-6%
5-7%
3-5%
9,394 ft

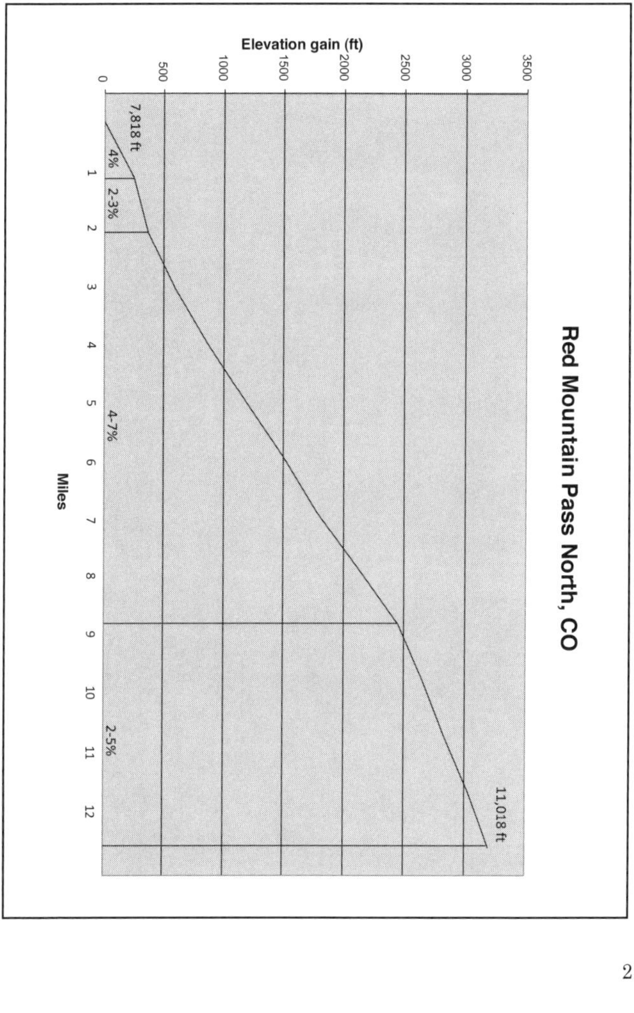
Red Mountain Pass North, CO
Elevation gain (ft)
0
500
1000
1500
2000
2500
3000
3500
Miles
1
2
3
4
5
6
7
8
9
10
11
12
7,818 ft
4%
2-3%
4-7%
2-5%
11,018 ft

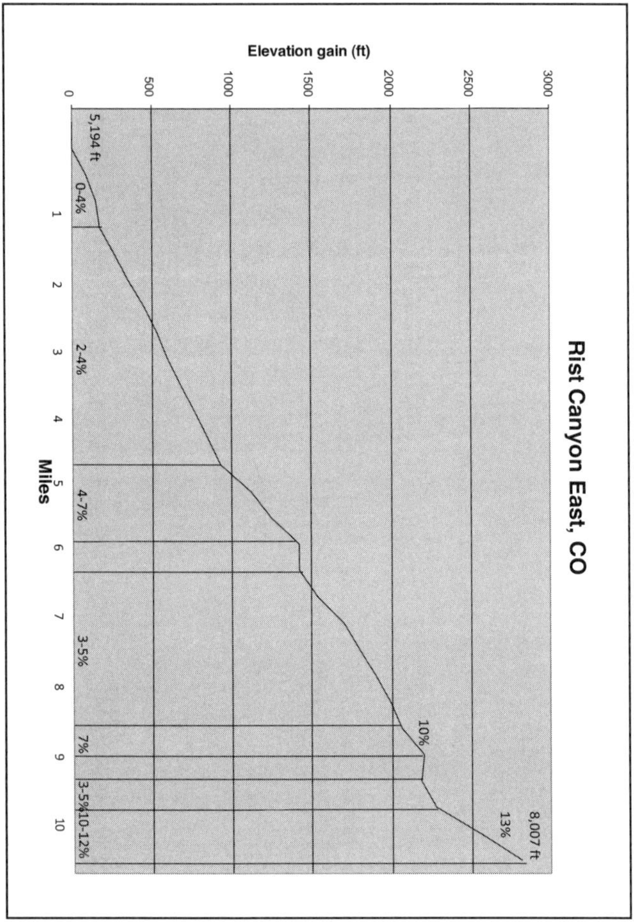
Rist Canyon East, CO
Elevation gain (ft)
0
500
1000
1500
2000
2500
3000
Miles
1
2
3
4
5
6
7
8
9
10
5,194 ft
0-4%
2-4%
4-7%
3-5%
10%
7%
3-5%
10-12%
13%
8,007 ft

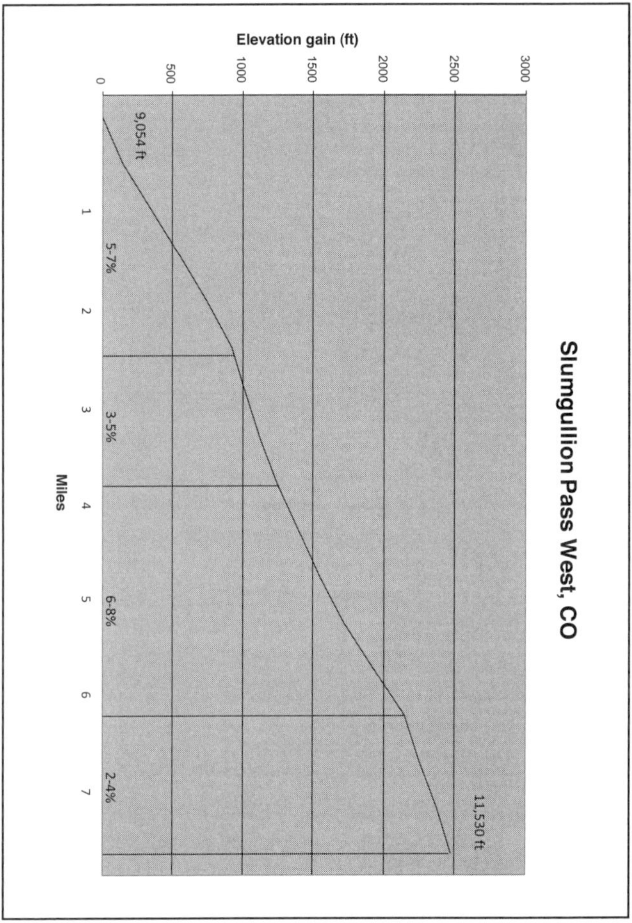

Slumgullion Pass West, CO
Elevation gain (ft)
0
500
1000
1500
2000
2500
3000
9,054 ft
11,530 ft
5-7%
3-5%
6-8%
2-4%
1
2
3
4
5
6
7
Miles

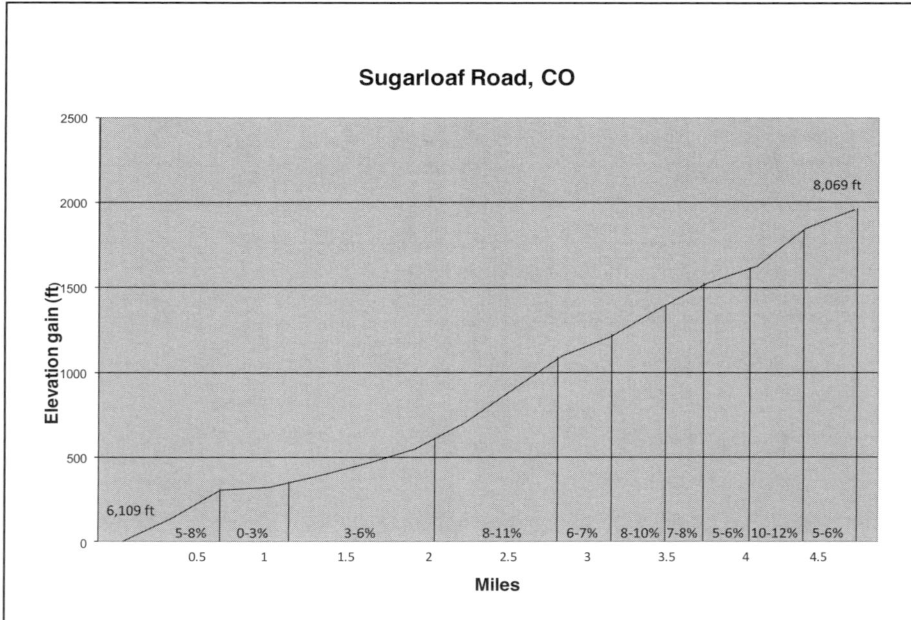
Sugarloaf Road, CO
Elevation gain (ft)
2500
2000
1500
1000
500
0
8,069 ft
6,109 ft
5-8%
0-3%
3-6%
8-11%
6-7%
8-10%
7-8%
5-6%
10-12%
5-6%
0.5
1
1.5
2
2.5
3
3.5
4
4.5
Miles

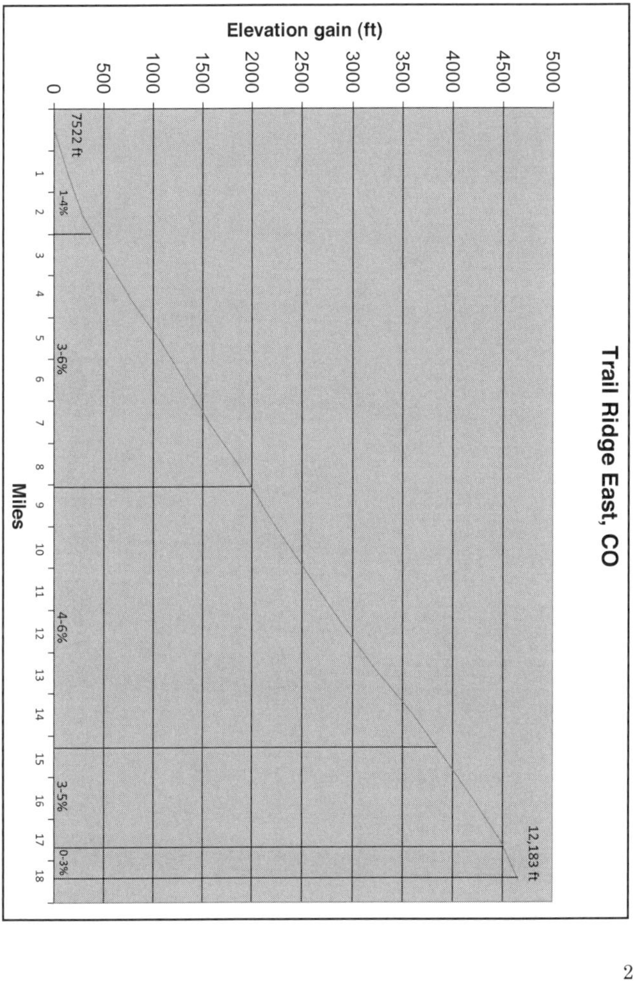
Trail Ridge East, CO
Elevation gain (ft)
0
500
1000
1500
2000
2500
3000
3500
4000
4500
5000
Miles
1
2
3
4
5
6
7
8
9
10
11
12
13
14
15
16
17
18
7522 ft
1-4%
3-6%
4-6%
3-5%
0-3%
12,183 ft

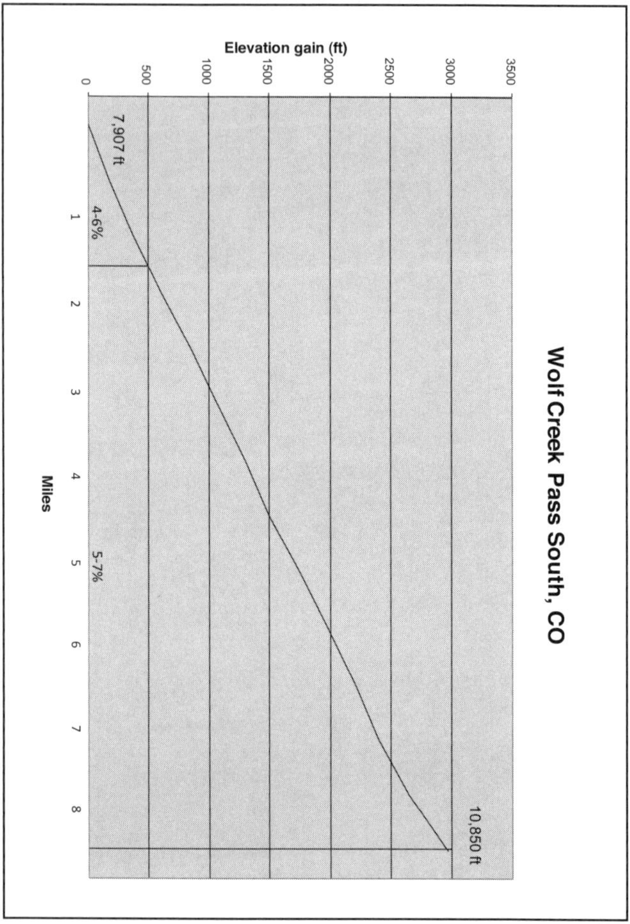
Wolf Creek Pass South, CO
Elevation gain (ft)
0
500
1000
1500
2000
2500
3000
3500
7,907 ft
4-6%
5-7%
10,850 ft
1
2
3
4
5
6
7
8
Miles

Index

Ominous weather and grade ahead